EXORCISING EMMA

Also by Margot Peters

Charlotte Brontë: Style in the Novel

Unquiet Soul: A Biography of Charlotte Brontë

Bernard Shaw and the Actresses

Mrs Pat: The Life of Mrs. Patrick Campbell

The House of Barrymore

May Sarton: A Biography

Wild Justice (as Margret Pierce)

Design for Living: Alfred Lunt and Lynn Fontanne

Summers: A True Love Story

Lorine Niedecker: A Poet's Life

Copyright © 2017 Margot Peters

EXORCISING EMMA

A Memoir

Margot Peters

much love (aka Flossie) to Gloria from Margo — (Bubbles)

Emma Klade Merkel, Margot's grandmother, in 1904

CHAPTER ONE

It's 1942. I'm nine years old, I finished Fourth Grade two weeks ago. I'm lying on my stomach in the back yard behind Grandmother's thorny rose bushes. My grandmother is Emma Klade Merkel, the Emma of this book title. I am praying that she can't spy me from her kitchen window. The grass is raw. Summer comes late up Wausau, Wisconsin-way, and bleeding hearts are just velveting into pink.

Most mornings start with the sun shooting arrows over East Hill. By noon, though, ranks of dark clouds shoulder in from the west. Right now low-flying shadows marble the grass. I tell time by the fingers of the lilac bush stretching long and longer across the lawn. It's got to be after three.

Whenever the sun goes under a cloud I suddenly feel the wind. *Why is that?* It's one of my puzzles. I have so many. Like the moon: sometimes it stands dead still, other times it flies across the sky like it's scared of its own white face. More important: Why don't I have a father? Sisters or brothers? Where is Grandfather? Above all: why are Mother and I trapped in Grandmother's house?

Why can't we leave?

This is my darkest puzzle of all.

I pluck a bleeding heart off the bush. With my thumbs I part its outer petals and they split into two pink rabbits. Magic! Next high-heeled slippers pop out, then a pair of drop earrings. Lastly, from flower's heart, I pluck a translucent milk bottle tipped with a gold star. Now five pleasingly-plump girls with naturally-curly hair and bobbing earrings can step into a magic coach pulled by rabbits and swig a bottle of milk on their way to the ball. *Voila!*

Mother flings lots of French about the house. She *adores* French, she *hates* German.

Her parents are German.

"*No!* Your grandfather's family came from Saxony, your great-grandmother's from Alsace-Lorraine. *And your father is a McCullough.*"

Oh, fiddle-de-de! (Could I have been just six when teachers herded our Central School elementary classes two blocks to the very Grand Theatre to see *Gone With the Wind*? First-graders got balcony seats. With so many boys stamping my feet as they went out to pee or buy candy, I took in only fragments of the film. It was so long it had an Intermission.)

Now, though, I'm devouring Judy Bolton mysteries and *Wuthering Heights* which has pledged me forever to wind-swept moors and black-haired gypsy-men who gnash their teeth for love of girls named Cathy. I'm also a Girl Scout. We meet in the Methodist Church basement—oops "lower level." Girl Scouts don't get to do cool Boy Scout things like go on hikes and carry knives and compasses and sleep in tents and roast wienies, and what a *drag* stitching the ten merit badges I've earned onto my uniform sleeve. Boy Scouts' mothers do it for them. Mother doesn't sew, but when her only sister Marie comes to Wausau she forces me into a chair with needle and thread. I speckle crisp fabrics with my life's blood. My touch is *death.*

Suddenly sunshine claps a friendly hand on my shoulder. I roll over, close my eyes, stretch. Hot cinnamon dances behind my eyelids. In the middle of each eye pulses a fiery red circle rimmed in black. Just like me, I think dramatically. A fiery little girl prisoned within a black ring of terror.

I have one of the few mothers in Wausau who works outside the home. She has to. Our fingers clamp the cliff-edge of poor. Mother proofreads for the *Wausau Daily Record Herald* from eight to four in a room narrow as a pencil and dark except for two sizzling fluorescent tubes over her slanted desk. She earns twenty-four dollars a week, no bennies. Unionized male typesetters make sixty-five, plus health care and retirement. Every Christmas, a *Record-Herald* boy delivers to Grandmother's back door a 24-pound turkey. Tucked under its wing is an unwritten message: "Don't complain." *And* Grandmother has to tip him.

At the end of Mother's room a tall window stares down on Fourth Street, a block from Central where I go to school. After school, I run to that window, jump onto a ledge and rap. Mother swivels in her chair. A deep frown that comes from staring all day at fine print bisects her pretty white forehead. Every night she sticks a Frownies patch between her eyebrows, though every morning the cleft is still there. I watch her size six toeless navy sling-backs approach the window. She squats sideways, locking knees so she won't show panties. She hoists the window three inches and shakes her head.

I know, I know. We can't afford a car, we can't afford a taxi. We can't afford enough winter coal or new gutters for the old house or even a fresh coat of paint. We can't afford train tickets to visit Aunt Marie in Milwaukee, we can't afford the corduroy "Autumn Flame" dress in Heineman's window I am dying for. We can't afford the fox stole in Winkelman's that Mother, posing before a dressing-room mirror, flips as casually as bathroom towel about her shoulders.

We *can* afford a ham salad sandwich at Vulling's Drugstore counter next door. Some months we can afford *Photoplay*.

"Cornell Wilde's on the cover, I love love love him, please please, Mother."

She opens her purse, shakes her head at my impossible extravagance, absolves me with a quarter.

I race to Mrs. Smith's shop three blocks away on Third Street. Mrs. Smith's is strange—long and dark like Mother's office, but filled with magazines and books and fruity aromas of candy and gum. White-haired Mrs. Smith sits behind the cash register, benevolent and huge as a mushroom—funny because her daughter Dixie's skinny, nervous, and dark. I cruise the narrow aisles. What to buy? *Photoplay* with slant-eyed Gene Tierney on the cover? A strawberry Dixie Cup? Yes! I rip off the lid, praying for the photo of Tyrone Power or Cary Grant. You have to lick off the ice-cream to see.

Always Gene Autry or Joe E. Brown.

A breeze shivers the raspberry leaves to silver. I scramble to my feet, check my white shorts: grass-stained. "Hell to pay!" Brassy sun paints the bellies of clouds still thickening in the west. Mother, hurry up! I have to pee and *I hate to go inside.* I squat behind a current bush, swab my crotch with a handful of the wispy grass that grows at the roots of apple trees. Mother should be at the railroad tracks by now, just starting the long climb up Washington Street.

I tear down the drive and drop into a spot below the arbor vitae that separate Emma's lot from the neighbors' below where I can see down past Tenth almost to Seventh. If only she'll come! I fiddle with jacks and a ball. Jacks are tricky on East Hill because my ball can be bouncing off railroad tracks before I swipe.

She's coming! The sun's at her back but I know it's her. She never hurries. Her legs are curved like commas and she deliberately places one foot in front of the other to mask the defect. It slows her down. Also, she's always alone.

In winter she wears a squirrel-trimmed wool coat that nips her waist before flaring to her knees. Her pillbox hat is squirrel too, she wears it tipped over her right eye. Her snow boots with fake-fur tops come half-way up her calves. But it's summer now, though cool, and I can see she's wearing the flowered dress she chose because the deceitful morning predicted warm weather. She hugs her arms, purse swinging like a pendulum across her stomach. She comes: a sleepwalker, a star, rising up Washington Street.

When she crosses Tenth I hurl myself into her arms. She smells of cigarettes and Jergen's. Her hands get filthy from proof ink, she always visits the Ladies to wash and cream before leaving work.

"Mmm," she says, pushing me off to look at me with cool blue eyes. She's not the cuddly type. She smiles, then droops her mouth.

"Hell to pay about those shorts."

Mother's so young and pretty and sad, I'd kill myself before giving her more to worry about.

"She won't find out."

Then she grins. "One more ciggy." She plants her shapely bum against an elm, shakes a Pall Mall out of a pack, frowns at the match she nails to the tip. She draws deeply, hollowing her cheeks. I'm enveloped in sophistication.

I can almost reach her.

I can't.

She shuts her eyes, she's somewhere else now. I wait. After only a year or two, she opens her eyes. She nods.

We lag up the block to Grandmother's house. I snap a few daisies, squat to examine a puss-green caterpillar inching hopefully across the walk. Below the arbor vitae hedge, Mother takes a last drag then spins away her cigarette with finger and thumb.

"Well, kiddo, here we go."

CHAPTER TWO

I am thirty years old before I find a photo of 1016 Washington Street in an ancient album. It is labeled "HAPPY HOME."

Jesus. What went on before I was born?

But today I am still only nine. We toss a coin. Heads side door, tails back. Heads.

"If she's in the kitchen," plots Mother, "we just head upstairs. If she's in the parlor, we grab from the ice box and eat al fresco."

I've figured out that "al fresco" means eating at the picnic table on the cement square poured one summer to floor a garage before the money ran out. Aunt Marie had purchased the table for the lawn in hopeful mood.

Emma's banging pans in the kitchen.

(I must make it clear about my calling her "Emma." As a child I addressed her, always, as "Grandmother." Writing twenty-five years after her death, I call her "Emma" because with the passage of time we are contemporaries. More than that, I still have an aversion to admitting she is my grandmother.)

We lift the side-door latch like thieves, glide up basement stairs, streak through the parlor, dart to our rooms.

The upstairs of Emma's house has three bedrooms. Emma's, in front, overlooks Washington Street. Mine is in the middle. Mother's is in back overlooking the garden.

I shut Mother's door tight. *Made it!*

But now that she's actually here, I feel absurdly let down.

She tosses her purse onto the bed, kicks off her shoes, wriggles the print dress over her head.

"What have you been up to all day, Miggles?"

"Stuff. Me and Helen played."

"Helen and *I* played. Me is *never* the subject of the verb, only its object."

"Helen and *I* played."

She swoons onto the bed in her peach slip, curls up like a leaf, tucks plump white hands under her chin, closes her eyes.

I *know* she works five days a week 8:30 to 5 and 9 to 2 on Saturday. But Mother, please stay awake just long enough to tell me what we're going to do about supper and the rest of the evening.

I sniff the air, can't smell supper. "Shall I go down and see?"

She yawns, sits up. Instead of answering, she rummages in her purse, hands me a flat package.

I stare.

"A Kotex belt. For when—*you know*."

I do know. All those cute ads promising slender blonde teen girls that they can swim, bowl and ski like Olympians "because with Kotex your secret is safe."

"*Mother!* I'm nine."

"Aunt Marie started at eleven, you never know."

"But I'm hungry."

"When's last time you've eaten?"

"Last year."

She swings white legs off the bed, disappears into her closet, comes out tying a blue chenille robe around her waist.

"I suppose we'll have to go down, Miggy."

Emma is hunched in her Windsor chair listening to the news on the Philco radio. We've been at war with Japan since December 7, 1941, I know because President Roosevelt interrupted my "Lone Ranger" radio program to talk about a day of infamy that would live forever. I didn't know what "infamy" meant, but I felt it must be bad. Strange, I'm only nine but I feel the War very personally.

As it turns out, I'm fascinated most by General MacArthur. In pictures he's always wearing sunglasses, which make him kind of sinister, and he smokes a corncob pipe that juts out between his clenched teeth farther than his jutting jaw. MacArthur is in the Pacific that has island names with lots of vowels, like Guadalcanal, Bataan, Leyte, Luzon, Iwo Jima, Okinawa. My third-grade teacher told us Pacific means "peace," but that makes no sense to me.

I know that some neighbors plant victory gardens at the top of Washington Street and save fats. We don't and I'm ashamed. Walking to school I pass houses with flags in their windows—two, three, even five stars that stand for how many sons are serving our country. We display one star because Uncle Johnny's in the war. Though Emma boasts, "He's with General Patton," Mother, Marie and I know Johnny's safe behind the lines in the Postmasters Corps, wrapping packages.

Three times a week Emma sends me to the grocery below the tracks with a rationing book. Mr. Schumacher is behind the counter. With cold fingers I slide our green ration book toward him. "Halleluiah, I'm a bum!" he shouts. *(Why?)* Today we don't have enough coupons for meat or sugar, but he doles out flour and butter. He rips green stamps out of our ration book, dings the cash register, shoves the book back at me. Shame floods me every time. We *never* have enough ration stamps. I scuttle out the door.

Now Mother adopts the false bright voice I know so well.

"Hello, Mother! Ginny sends love as always."

Emma doesn't glance over her shoulder, we're not worth it. She leans forward and cranks the volume higher.

"Thought you'd died and gone to heaven. Table's set. Don't like my cooking you can telegraph that husband of mine to come home, fix a meal once in his life."

"Daddy's supporting us," Mother ventures, quickly adding, "We'll love whatever you make." A glaring falsehood. We will not love whatever Emma makes. Her cooking is deliberately noxious. I think it's her way of hating her husband—and us.

One hot summer day two or three years ago, I'm sitting at the desk in the stifling front parlor so humid the walls are damp to my touch—trying to write a thank-you note to Aunt Marie. Emma's thick grey-black hair is climbing wildly toward the ceiling like a vine.

"*Why* did I marry your grandfather? Because he was a chef. Chefs *cook*, am I right? *All that man does* is pinch the turkey leg once a year at Thanksgiving to see if it's done."

I think Grandfather's got guts just entering Emma's kitchen.

"He makes chicken fricassee" I say loyally, mouth watering as I remember tender chicken in rich gravy over flaky biscuits.

"*Why* do you remember that chicken fricassee?" She lowers her head to glare at me, glasses sliding down her nose. "I'll tell you. Because he made it *once,* that's why."

Emma never sits down at table with us, not even for holidays. She shoves open the dining room door with a hip, dumps plates of food on the table, retreats to her kitchen stool. Such a small stool for such a large woman, ordered from a Sears Roebuck catalogue: yellow vinyl with padded back, black rubber steps.

Always they send me to the kitchen on food errands. I might find her gnawing a bone like an animal, or maybe sitting at the window table, face pressed against the pane as though she'd like to smash it and eat the shards. Her bulk is huge, but I seldom see her eat. Another of my puzzles. Does she eat all day while we're gone? Nights while we sleep?

I must be exaggerating, but I can't remember eating a meal in Emma's house that sat easy on my stomach.

Mornings she flings oatmeal into our bowls, slams them on the kitchen table in front of us. Once I pushed away my bowl because she had burned the oatmeal. She cuffed me so hard my head looked over my left shoulder.

When Emma raves she puffs up into a toad five times larger than the woman who weighs 200 pounds. I've seen her cranking up, spurring herself on until she morphs from a handsome woman into a monster of rage, spitting out hatred like sinew, flesh and bone. Her mouth foams, her saliva spatters my face.

Suck-tit, crack-fucker, tit boy, cock-sucker, bung-boy, cunt-fuck....

Theoretically, I am being raised in a respectable middle-class family. Aunt Marie is an educator in Milwaukee. Mother works for the local newspaper. Grandfather is a chef at the Hotel Merrill. Uncle Johnny is a glamorous playboy out East.

But we are not respectable inside Emma's house because she does not respect us.

I live with a Monster bent on devouring her kin.

We must have eaten that evening, I remember doing dishes, trying not to rattle plates, tiptoeing upstairs. Mother unzips her manicure set and buffs her nails. She's reading a novel called *The Ivory Mischief.* I have a new Judy Bolton mystery. On the dust jacket a sinister man seems unaware that Judy is spying on him from behind a gnarled oak. This latest addition to my potentially definitive Judy Bolton Library cost me 65 cents yesterday at Janke's Book Store on Third Street. Janke's is my favorite Wausau store. I have written in blue-black Scrip ink on the title page "This

Book Belongs to Margo McCullough" because I've run out of the book plates Aunt Marie gave me that show a young woman with high curls and a low neckline gazing out a window, a book clasped in her hands. Aunt Marie *fanatically* gives me books, I *fanatically* read them.

But it's not over for the day that began with Helen and me (Helen and *I)* playing, then me—*I*—lying on my stomach plucking bleeding hearts and waiting for Mother.

First I hear a low rumble, like Indians beating tom-toms. Then I catch a few words.

"Doing dirty with the neighbor boys."

This is familiar, this can pass. I slide a bookmark into Judy, cross the hall to the bathroom, drop my white shorts into the dirty clothes pile in the walk-in closet. Back in my room I shrug on the pink robe with my initials embroidered on the collar, MMM. Aunt Marie gave it to me for my last birthday on May 13 instead of books.

When I'm really scared, when I've shoved a chair under the door knob so that Emma can't burst into my room (though she can anyway), I kneel in front of the window and breathe on the pane.

In the mist I draw a six-point star. Not really a six-point star, but my personal fortress: my initials MMM in a circle. Three solid *M* bases to protect my body and soul, six spikes aimed to impale intruders.

But it's summer so there's no order to my days, except Emma's raving. I crave order, I crave homework, not homework exactly: a *mission*.

Now she's on the landing.

"Think you're wanted, don't you! Let me tell you, your mother snuck to an abortionist, that's how much she cared about you. Your father, that cunt-sucker, didn't try to stop her. So what does that make you, hoor-spawn, what does that make you?"

I squeeze shut my eyes, willing blindness to bring deafness as well. Blindness does not cooperate. I burrow deeper into the covers, jam a finger in each ear. I can still hear her, but now her voice is like waves smashing against rocks far below an ocean cliff. Not that I've ever seen an ocean cliff, but I've seen a movie of one.

I don't cry. I never cry. If I cry, Emma wins.

I'm too young to have heard Franklin Delano Roosevelt's famous Fireside Chat during the Great Depression when he assured America, "We have nothing to fear but fear itself." But if I'd heard him, his words would not have helped.

I am a child and there is no remedy for childhood except growing up. And I can't grow up, not right away. I am afraid.

CHAPTER THREE

In 1981 I married for a third time—at last, happily. I found myself hanging a portrait of the young Emma over my bed.

I want to know why. Because I may as well kiss a cottonmouth as hang Emma Merkel on my wall.

The photographer's head was buried under a cloth, isn't that how they used to do it? Chin high, scornful Emma looks past him, hands clasped behind a straight back. A straw hat rides her black curls. Her nose repeats the prow of the hat. Her eyes are shadowed. I knew them to be that witchy flecking of brown and green called hazel. Her mouth is arrogant and tender, her neck a white column.

A society beauty—except I can tell that her black shirtwaist dress and hat are cheap. Emma is nineteen. The year is 1904, twenty-nine years before she became my grandmother. In the photograph her hair is growing back after scarlet fever.

Sometimes she talks to me; well, I'm the only one there to listen. She leans forward, her Windsor chair groaning. I'm probably seven or eight.

"I near died of scarlet fever. My mother shaved my head with my father's straight razor because the doctor said my heavy hair was draining my strength. When my black hair grew back it was thick and curly. All the boys went crazy 'cause I was the only girl in town with short curls."

This reminds me of the story famous in our family. The wealthy Judd Alexander invited young Emma to a party.

"My mother sewed me an evening gown of yellow silk." She's drinking black Hills Brothers coffee that's been curing in a pan on the stove since five a.m. "I hadn't a jot of jewelry so I trimmed my dress with green leaves and red ribbons. Every man in the room danced with me that night except Judd. The last waltz was called and still he hadn't glanced my way. Then I knew he'd invited me only to shame me. I ran out his front door and down his steps. I stopped, looking for something to destroy as he'd destroyed me. I ripped up calla lilies, I smashed two urns."

I didn't doubt her.

"Remember: it's just as easy to marry a rich man as a poor one."

"Then why didn't you, Grandmother?"

Her blow knocks me off my chair.

She has no friends, she lets nobody inside the house, that's why she talks to me. She leans forward, wafting sweat and lilac perfume. "I'll whisper you a secret. My sister Minnie's half Indian." (She doesn't know the term Native American, nobody did then.) "Why do you think she bought her own beauty parlor? Because she was crazy to perm straight Indian hair.'

"Minnie Indian?" I say doubtfully, clearly seeing Minnie's dead-straight black hair, high-bridged nose, warrior cheekbones.

"My mother Wilhelmina was raped half-dead by a Chippewa chief. Any fool can see Minnie's half Indian."

Emma has many Indian stories. I love Indian stories!

"I spent days at my grandparents' farm because they were good to me. One morning they left for town in the buggy. I was hungry for a bowl of cornmeal mush with maple syrup. I'd never made mush but I boiled a pot of water on the wood stove and threw in three or four handfuls. Pretty soon the mush was bumping the lid so I snatched another pot and poured in half but the mush bubbled over that pot, so I grabbed another.

"Then something shivered in my bones. I looked over my shoulder. Two Indian faces were pressed against the window! I screamed."

"Did they wear war paint, did they have scalps on their belts!"

Emma snorts, I'm spoiling her story.

"They pushed into the kitchen. 'Food,' they said, all the English they could speak."

"'No food!'

"They pointed at the pots boiling over on the stove. I fetched three bowls, herding the Indians from the kitchen, banged the bowls down on the stoop and slammed the door after them, my heart going like sixty. When I dared look again the pots were licked clean and the Indians had vanished."

"Did they have bows and arrows?"

She heaves her bulk out of the chair, spitting with disgust. "Talking to you's like talking to the deaf, only worse."

But I believe her, just as I can picture her in downtown Wausau on the boardwalk dodging the tobacco spit of Indians squatting in their blankets against the hardware store. That was long, long ago.

I'm twenty-seven when my mother says, apropos of nothing: "You know you're part Indian, don't you?"

"Is that why I walk pigeon-toed?" I say foolishly.

She lights another cigarette, not interested in how I walk. "Your father's grandfather married an Indian woman."

"What tribe?"

"Wisconsin."

"Menomonee, Chippewa, Winnebago, Potawatomi, Sac?" We studied Indians in fourth grade.

She shrugs and I do nothing with this information. My heritage is a mystery I don't need to solve. I survived, that's enough.

I am poring over a 1903 studio portrait of the five sisters. Emma, Minnie, Ida, Hattie, and Elsie—names that evoke green lawns, slow afternoons, shady hats. Though they are all dressed in virgin white, they don't look alike. Emma the eldest is womanly at eighteen, the only sister allowed to wear a large black hair bow.

Sly Ida stands behind her, even prettier than Emma. Minnie looks defiant, her thin, black-stockinged legs and Emma's black bow the only contrast in the photo. Blond Hattie looks faintly worried, perhaps anticipating Emma's rage. Elsie, my black-haired, fiery-tempered Great-Aunt, is still unformed, characterless, the youngest. Though Emma named my mother after Elsie her sister, I cannot remember her uttering a good word about any of her sisters. Calling Minnie half-Indian was almost a compliment.

"My parents spoiled my four younger sisters but worked me like a slave. When Hattie, that sugar-mouth snake, married no-good Jim Allen—"

I cross my fingers behind my back because I often sneak up the hill to visit 1202 Washington. The Allens' pretty white house sits on a corner lot, green lawns lorded over by giant white pines. Their front door is welcoming, their windows sparkle. Compared to Hattie's, Emma's house looks bleakly uninviting. The difference is planted deep in Emma's heart. I remember finding her once on her knees in the garden planting gooseberries because she'd heard that gooseberries blight white pines.

Emma would kill me if she knew I go up the hill to the Allens.

Just a year ago I got new information about the warring sisters from Hattie's youngest daughter and my favorite cousin, Pat Ann. When Hattie and Jim lived in Blackwell, Wisconsin, in northwest Forest County, Emma sent her three children by train summer after summer to visit. Hattie said they arrived in dirty ragged clothes that she washed and mended. Allen photos of Marie, John and my mother Elsie prove Emma sent them on the train to Hattie. *Emma and Hattie were close.* Then Hattie returned to Wausau and built a pretty house with their father's money two blocks higher than Emma's on Washington Street, a "betrayal" that permanently dyed Emma's heart black against Hattie.

"Built higher up the hill *so she could look down on me.* Your grandfather and I crawled on our knees for a mortgage not paid to this day. My father did nothing for us. Always Hattie, Hattie—"

From her post at the front window where she sits drinking her lethally strong Hills Brothers coffee, Emma spots Hattie walking down the hill. The sight of her slender, favored sister sends her surging onto the porch.

"*Snake-shit*" Emma hurls down the hill after Hattie's quickly receding back. "*Piss-sucker!*"

Where did she learn such filth?

"My father had the Devil's own tongue."

She is sitting in the Windsor chair, a wedding present for her marriage in 1905. She has raved for hours. Spittle crusts the corners of her mouth. But it's early June and lilac breeze billows the sheer curtains and, weirdly enough, Emma is temporarily at peace. She hands me a glass from a tray ."Lemonade, made in the shade, frogs at the bottom, but don't be afraid." Emma abhors frogs.

I try to imagine her girlhood. She was gifted, she wrote poetry in secret. I can hear her father's heavy boots on narrow stairs, the crash of bedroom door against wall. Emma, sixteen, has been writing in a notebook given her by her fifth-grade teacher. Her father tears it out of her hands. The night is shattered by his blows and curses. I imagine Emma turning her head away, refusing to cry.

August Klade, the great-grandfather I never really knew—I was too afraid of him—had a blacksmith shop behind the white clapboard house on Forest Street in one of Wausau's oldest residential areas, down by the tracks. Once when I seven or eight, I visited Forest Street alone. That day he led me out of the house to the disused shop that I saw was collapsing from rot on its north side. When Great-Grandfather heaved back the door, the sharp smell of horse dung and rusting iron flew up and bit my nostrils. Straps and harnesses festooned the walls, in the dark I could make out what he said was an anvil. He'd given up blacksmithing long ago.

"Our Father licked us girls black and blue." Hattie on one of my secret visits. "But your grandmother Emma got it worst. Father had it in for Emma. He'd drag by her long black hair kicking and fighting out back to his blacksmith shop."

"*Why* did he hate my Grandmother, Aunt Hattie?"

She shakes her white head. Once her hair was black, like all the sisters.' "Before Emma was born, twin boys died, three days old. I always thought Father took out their deaths on Emma."

Occasionally Emma takes me downtown to shop. In summer she wears a hat, a dark flower-print dress, and white shoes. She walks deliberately, her feet turned out in the style of her youth. To the few people she deigns to notice she gives a brief nod. My cheeks burn. We're nobody, why is she pretending we are?

We start with The Fair Store, a huge retail cavern with worn wooden floors, counters piled with pokey merchandise, the reek of unsold cloth. Just the store for Emma, who refused to buy a refrigerator until the day the iceman parked his horse and wagon in front of 1016 Washington and knocked at the back door, tongs gripping the melting block of ice hoisted onto his padded leather shoulder. "Last delivery, Mrs. Merkel. Goin' out of business. Nobody but you takes ice anymore." The iceman goeth.

Emma is tall, I am small. I follow her through miles of Fair Store aisles. The counters are above my head. When she pays for a corset or a length of cloth, a clerk stuffs her crumpled dollar bills into a metal container, presses a switch and sends the box sizzling up a wire to the second-floor office, where a hand hauls in the cash and sends the box zooming back with change and a receipt. The ground floor buzzes like a bee hive.

Sometimes we go to Kresge's Five & Ten. Emma may give me a dime to buy Crayolas or Princesses Elizabeth and Margaret paper dolls. I love Princess Elizabeth and Princess Margaret! I can dress them in riding habits or blue satin dresses with white fur and tiaras atop their curls. I am *dying* to get home and cut them out. But, like an after-thought, Emma leads the way to the lunch counter and drops her bulk onto a red-plastic stool, salivating at the thought of what she's going to order. Three times a week she sends me down to the store below the tracks to buy strawberry ice cream, I've seen her lick up a quart in minutes. Now she orders a chocolate, strawberry and butter pecan banana split, topped with hot fudge, caramel, butterscotch, whipped cream, nuts, and a cherry. She holds her spoon with her little finger cocked as though she's doing the banana split a favor. Finally she puts down her spoon and pats her lips with the small paper napkin. I make a loud noise with my straw at the bottom of my chocolate soda. "Disgusting," she says.

Next we might go to Mayer's, the best shoe store in town.. I adore new shoes, this should be a super-special occasion. Alas. Though Emma herself buys shoes from catalogues, she insists on choosing mine. We enter a hushed, carpeted room, we take seats.

"How may I serve you?" A bald smiling man bends over me.

"Patent-leather Mary Janes," I whisper.

"Oxfords," corrects Emma.

He unties my saddle shoes. Why do my shoes instantly turn into garbage in a shoe store, even when they're not all that old? One of my puzzles. I kick them under my chair. The man returns, balancing five boxes under his chin. He kneels at my feet, pops a box, brings forth a shoe smelling of pure new leather. I inhale greedily. Using a silver shoe horn he slips it over my white anklets.

"Now we'll check the fit." He escorts me to a big machine, directs me to slide a foot into a tunnel, presses a switch. I look down and see my green bones glowing through the shoes like reeds in a pond.

He shakes his head. "The shoe barely fits now. Look how her second toe is pushing the leather. We'll try the next size up."

"We'll take these."

"But, Ma'am—"

"*No, Grandmother, please don't buy these shoes, they pinch me already.*"

"Wrap them up."

I remember my feet before Emma. "You will be a ballet dancer," says Aunt Marie, caressing and stretching my toes. "Your second toe is longer than your big toe—that's what ballet dancers need for balance."

I would never become a ballet dancer. But Emma deliberately crippled me.

"Ladies have small feet."

Crazy! Emma's mail-order shoes were size ten.

Emma loved the Wisconsin Valley Fair at the Marathon Park Fairgrounds. After one excursion, we are photographed (by Marie? Johnny?) standing in front of 1016 with our loot. Emma flourishes a paddle-ball, Grandfather a jumbo jar of coffee, me a book.

We probably went to the Fair more than once, but one time stamps itself on my memory. Emma and I are strolling toward the big building that houses pens of fragrant animals as well as displays of women's needlework, gladioli, jarred pickles, and homemade pies. A hot wind from the race track spins dust into our eyes. As usual, Emma wears a print dress, straw hat, white shoes. We are making our way slowly toward the Exposition Building when I see a tall, dark man walking toward us.

I stop, I don't know why.

I've seen tons of movies, but this man beats any star. He's walking between two women. They're outlines, only the man in focus. His thick black hair is combed back from a widow's peak. His shirt is as white as God. His cuffs are rolled above tanned forearms. He wears a thick black watch on his left wrist.

He stops when he sees us.

Emma jerks me away so violently that I feel my shoulder leave its socket. She whirls me past the Midway and zigzags between tents poles until we reach the picnic tables under the tall white pines. She sinks panting onto a bench and flaps a cardboard fan stamped FAIR DEAL HARDWARE at her scarlet face.

"Who was *that*?" I ask fearfully.

"That? *That was The Devil!*"

CHAPTER FOUR

I live at 1016 Washington Street in Wausau with my Grandmother Emma Wilhelmina Klade Merkel. Though I always call her Grandmother, I think of her as Emma, hoping we're not truly related. My mother Elsie McCullough also lives in Emma's house, and sometimes my Grandfather, John Merkel.

The fact that I was born into Emma's Wausau is crucial. Emma is obsessed with wealthy Wausau and her young, wrong-side-of-the-tracks poverty. As Emma tells it, Wausau is a city of Rich and Poor. Betweens do not exist.

Wausau is the largest city of the largest county, Marathon, in north-central Wisconsin. Before I was born, white pines soaring to a hundred and fifty-feet covering the valley watered by the Wisconsin, Eau Pleine, Big Sandy and Big and Little Rib rivers. White hunters and trappers threaded fragrant forests punctuated by Chippewa village clearings. They traded with the Chippewa, not infrequently mated. These pines are relevant to my story.

When in 1839 an Easterner named George Stevens came to the valley, he saw that the pines meant millions and built the first mill on the banks of the Wisconsin River at Big Bull Falls. In 1845 he was followed by Walter McIndoe, also a hustler but a settling kind of man. He bought Stevens's mills, eventually changed the name Big Bull Falls to Wausau.

"Once a great Indian chief stood atop Rib Mountain," says Marie, my tall, nervous, and successful aunt currently wearing a yellow smock over summer slacks because she's painting wicker. "His name was Chief Wau. And all the land to the north, south, east and west he called The Land that Wau Saw." (Ouch.)

Nobody's sure about local place names. Did trappers name the rapids because they roar like a bull, or because French for rapids is *bulle?* Did the Chippewa really confide to McIndoe that on their yearly hunts they went "wausau"—far away? Or did they call Big Bull Falls "wausau" meaning "noise like thunder," since that word exists in at least one Wisconsin Indian language? What's sure is that Walter McIndoe was the founding spirit of the town that grew up along the east and west banks of the Wisconsin River.

When word flashed back East that big pines meant big money, men like Walter Alexander, Cyrus Yawkey, Alexander Stewart, and Walter Bissell also headed for Wisconsin. In 1892 these tycoons culled some four billion board-feet from the pinery, making Wisconsin the nation's leading producer of lumber.

But by 1905, when Emma was twenty, these men had reduced the pinery to stumps. Some took the money and ran. Alexander, Stewart and Yawkey decided to stick with Wausau. Strangling competition, the "Wausau Group" snapped up paper mills, electric companies and railways. Walter Alexander was the richest man in town. These lumber barons built their mansions on Grand Avenue or just off Main (Third) Street at Fourth and Fifth. McIndoe Street was prime.

Later-comers raced to the hill that rises east of the Milwaukee Road railroad tracks to end high above the city at Fourteenth Street, with gleaming views of Lake Wausau snuggling Rib Mountain.

Emma was born on Forest Street, outer boundary of the original city plat, not far from downtown and a block west of the tracks. As often happens, oldest residential areas decay fastest.

Emma's generation lusted for East Hill. But, as she drilled me, "There's East Hill and *East Hill*."

Had Emma stood at her attic window on tiptoe, she might have viewed the neighborhood she coveted to the north. Turning east, she could shake her fist at her sister Hattie's house built two blocks above her own. But she had no need to climb to the attic. A map of East Hill was buried in her heart. She did everything in her power to bury it in mine.

CHAPTER FIVE

I'm not sure, but I think that outing to the Wisconsin Valley Fair might have been the last time Emma left the house on her own. She gave up walking the five blocks downtown to the Fair Deal or Kresge's Five & Ten. Eventually she refused to go outdoors at all in the daytime, waiting until sunset or just before dawn to steal into her garden. Once a year she laced herself into a salmon-pink Lane Bryant corset and ordered her son Johnny to drive her down Grand Avenue to Pine Grove Cemetery so she could visit her parents' graves.

Why did she stop going out of the house? Today we would analyze agoraphobia, paranoia. As a child I guessed she felt intense shame of her body. She had been a beauty, she was proud. Later I wondered whether it might be shyness, too? Guilt? Hatred of the world she had almost conquered when young?

Mother seldom told me anything I really wanted to know. After her death in 2002, I re-connected with my mother's high school friend, Ginny Haase. I quizzed her endlessly about the past.

"You must have known my father."

"I never knew Edgar, sweetheart, I don't think I ever had a conversation with him."

"But you and Elsie were best friends."

"Guess I was too absorbed in Leon." She fidgets her wheelchair back and forth with thin, blue-veined hands. She doesn't want to talk about my father. "Ask me something else, Sweetheart."

We look at scrapbooks, photos of her family, I find half a dozen snapshots of *me*. So I existed, I'm real, I'm part of somebody's past. Mother's there too. In one photo she's lying on a rug on the grass, arm flung over her eyes, face lifted to the sky. I saw her so often that way: inviting dreams and oblivion.

"What about my grandmother?"

"Lovely woman! What good times we had. We'd pile into a flivver with our skis and dare the driver to make it up East Hill. Sometimes he did. Then we'd ski down and trek back up a dozen times. When we finally knocked at her house looking like Eskimos, Mrs. Merkel flung open the door and laughed. She always had a big pot of chili on the stove and hot chocolate with peppermints to thaw us out. After that came big warm slabs of gingerbread with whipped cream. Then we'd all gather at the piano and sing."

We cannot be talking about the same woman.

"Ginny, wait. My grandmother served Elsie's friends chili and gingerbread with whipped cream?"

"Golly, yes. She was hospitality itself."

Then I remember a photo of 1016 Washington Street stuck into silver triangles on a rough black album page and labeled "Happy Home."

What happened to Emma Merkel? All my life I've tortured myself with that question, I'm asking it now. What was it she hated so lethally? What was her open wound? When did she change? Am I the person who turned Happy Home into Hell House?

Without hanging out a shingle, I've become a detective of my own past. What clues exist to solve this mystery?

Could her father who beat her in his smithy have turned her against men forever? I never saw Emma and her father together, not even in old sepia photographs. When Mother, Aunt Marie, Uncle Johnny and I went to Forest Street for Christmas Day, Emma always stayed home.

"My mother's life was Hell on Earth," said Emma. What made Wilhelmina's life "Hell on Earth"—her husband? By the time I was twelve, August Klade lurched on two canes, head swinging side to side like a horse's being led to the knackers. Most of his teeth were gone. His house swarmed with active women cleaning, baking casseroles, decorating Christmas trees, wrapping presents. They extinguished him. He looked on, a beggar at his own feast. Yet I remember his blacksmith's shop and how I was afraid of him and what he did to Grandmother. Maybe Great-Grandmother was afraid of him too.

"Your grandmother could have married any rich man in town": Mother. I laugh skeptically, a word I don't know. How does the daughter of a blacksmith, raised on Forest Street below the tracks, confirmed in the German Lutheran Church, forced to drop out of school after sixth grade to labor at home—how could she have married any rich man in town?

But at that time, I hadn't seen a photograph of young Emma, the local beauty with the haughty chin, short black curls, and provoking mouth.

Though I'd listened to her stories.

"I was invited to hayrides and picnics and box socials. I had a pure contralto voice and sang with the Tuesday Music Club. I was snubbed, of course, by the snotty Ladies Literary Club and Monday Evening Study Group. Oh, no: I wasn't good enough by a long shot for the likes of *them*."

It's a wild wet day with bursts of sleet rattling the windows. March is coming in like a lion so will go out like a lamb, one of my certainties not my puzzles. I'm lying on the living room sofa tucked among Emma's afghans. From my invalid's couch I can read the back of the yellow poster stuck to our window:

CHICKEN POX

KEEP OUT

Though my red blisters are losing their putrescent glow, it'll be another week before I'm allowed back in school. Mornings, stinky neighborhood boys rush the porch steps, flatten their noses against the window, roll their eyeballs and run like sheep as Emma lunges for the front door.

"Why were they snotty to you?"

"Nasty word! Why waste my breath on you? Wausau's either East Hill or Nowhere."

"But we live on East Hill."

She laughs, grabs her jar of Vaseline and bends forward to unwind a bandage. Her tightly-muscled calves have gone bad supporting her 200-plus pounds. Purple wounds on her calves ooze yellow puss. I look away.

"The famous acting family, the Winningers, invited me to perform at Columbia Hall on Grand Avenue, next to the Ruder Brewery. After I did a scene from *Du Barry,* Mayor Kickbusch called me 'Our Local Sarah Siddons.' And before Charlie Winninger left town he begged me on his knees to go with him to New York . . ."

Such ancient history. My eyes close. With luck I won't wake until Mother comes home with a new Connect-the-Dots, though what I really crave are forbidden Bat Man and Wonder Woman comics.

"Your grandmother had dozens of suitors."

It's summer. I'm lying on my back on the blue bed in her blue room, arms under my head, staring at the blue ceiling while she enters names in the blue address book Marie gave her for Christmas. A breeze listlessly fingers the sheer curtains. Mother's two windows look out across the alley into big yards with mock-orange and lilac bushes, stone walls, and martin houses on tall tall poles. I *love* watching martins swoop and dive, I wish I were a martin.

"A young man named Fred, who lived at a good address on Sturgeon Eddy Road, made her swear to wait for him until he came home from military training."

"Who was Charlie?"

My mother screws the cap on her pen and sighs. "Your grandmother could have married Charles Winninger, he was daft about her."

"Who *was* he?"

"The actor, silly. Played Cap'n Andy in *Showboat* on Broadway, it ran 600 performances. When the movie came to Wausau a few years back, your grandmother refused to see it because she knew *she* could have played Magnolia Hawks."

I bounce up, finally impressed. So if Grandmother had left town with Charles Winninger, she'd be a famous actress today and we'd be living in New York or Hollywood.

Years later I do the math. Emma was born in 1885; in 1927, the year *Show Boat* opened on the Great White Way, she would have been forty-two. Just the right age for Winninger to play Cap'n Andy, *not* for Emma to play his daughter, Magnolia Hawks.

But wait! He'd asked her to come to New York years before, when she was a girl of seventeen. Even then he knew she was made for the stage. Oh, Emma, Emma, why didn't you go!

"But she didn't leave with Charlie because of Judd Alexander."

What is Judd Alexander compared to Charles Winninger? One day Emma tells me how they met.

"I was clerking at Wausau's best bakery that specialized in Vienna Torte, Mocha Cream Rolls, and French Kisses." She swipes at the moisture beading at the corners of her lips. "One day in walks Judd Alexander, fair as the Angel Gabriel, lumber Baron heir. I wrap him a loaf of bread with shaking hands.

"Next day he comes back and orders two French Kisses.

"When I told my mother I was going to marry him she slapped my face. 'Fool! Marry an Alexander? His family will spit on your shoes, they'll trample you like dirt. You'll make him miserable and he'll make you. Is that what you hanker for: a life of misery?' We were putting up rhubarb I'd just cut from the garden. I slammed down my jar and ran out of the house. I walked and walked. I gave up Judd but I never forgave my mother."

Meanwhile, John Ernest Merkel, the young man doomed to be my grandfather, had caught a train with the vague notion that adventure and profit lay somewhere west of Holyoke, Massachusetts. Once he told me that when the train pulled into

Chicago, he'd stepped onto the platform and tossed a nickel. Buffalo side up, he'd push on further west; Indian head, he'd catch the train north to Wisconsin.

Indian head, poor sod. I suppose not de-training until Wausau instead of Milwaukee, Portage or Stevens Point were also flips of the coin.

He's the same height as Emma (five-feet-nine) and poor, but he's from the East: a soft-spoken gentleman who refuses second helpings with, "I've had a grand sufficiency." Only occasionally he betrays his German heritage by saying things like *tanks* for *thanks.*

I try to imagine how they met. At the west-side Lutheran church, where good Germans prayed to *Heilege Gott?* At the Bon Ton when he smiled at her over a slice of Viennese Torte? At the counter of the once-famous "Fancy Grocer" at 401 Washington Street, where Emma clerked for owner Henry Oswald?

I'm guessing, since he's a cook, he's hired by a restaurant. One day she walks in. Not yet a chef, he waits on tables in a clean white apron. His blond hair is parted down the middle, his eyes are blue and mild, he sports a blond mustache. He is deferential. Still suffering from the Judd Alexander humiliation, she conquers swiftly. They are married in 1905. John is properly solemn on their wedding photo; Emma looks like a strong mare that doesn't intend to be broken.

"And poor Fred never married," sighs Mother, finishing her tale—but with none of the anguish she mourns J. A.

At the age of ten, I (obnoxiously) pride myself on being sensible. "If Grandmother had married Judd Alexander," I say briskly, "you and I wouldn't exist." She frowns at me. It is, apparently, a new thought.

I know very little about Emma and John's early married life, but I have clues.

Clue 1: A note in Uncle John's dashing hand, "Our father was a first-class chef who owned his own restaurant, The Model Cafe, until it was closed because of a depression in 1908."

Clue 2: A photograph of The Crystal Cafe, my grandfather's second restaurant in downtown Wausau. He poses solemnly, elbow on front counter, hand on hip. Hanging gas lamps light the Cafe. Behind the counter loom enormous urns for coffee, tea, and hot water. A brass cash register decorated with fleur-de-lis registers "Amount Received: 25 cents." Nine tables with white cloths, a bonnet and two bowlers hanging on racks, a cast-iron stove, a sideboard. A dark-haired young woman in a white apron and a blouse punctuated by a black tie stands against the back wall. It is Emma. She does not look happy.

Clue 3: A Crystal Cafe menu in my grandfather's elegant script. In 1907, for sixty cents, a customer can order Chicken Broth with Dumplings, Oysters, Relishes, Stuffed Turkey with Cranberry Sauce, Whipped Potatoes, Candied Yams, Creamed Golden Waxed Beans, Vegetable Jello Salade, Fresh Hot Rolls, and a choice of Mince, Lemon, Pumpkin or Apple Pie.

I'm so proud! *My* grandfather owned the Crystal Cafe in downtown Wausau! I treasure his hand-written 1911 St. Patrick's Day menu. Forty-five cents will buy Potage Erin Go Braugh, O'Neil's Relish, Toasted Shillahah's and Jigg's Corned Beef and Cabbage, McGettigan's Ham with Muldoon's Hoe Cake and Galway Sauce, Creamed Banty Chick wit' Widdy Murphy's Cream Sauce, Irish Rosettes, Emeralds in Cream, Shamrock Rolls, Mollie McGuire's Green Apple Pie with Bridget Shailla's Churned Cow, Blackthorn Coffee and Red-Eye Tay.

Emma must have murdered his charming sense of fun before I made his acquaintance.

Mother rolls over onto her stomach.

"World War One, you can't imagine the hatred against Germans. Mr. Schultz next door taught his son to "Salut the Kaiser" by thumbing his nose. Every German in town was scared."

Suddenly I understand my mother's passionate pursuit of French, my aunt's deep delve into British literature, my Uncle John's Cary Grant accent and cosmopolitan chic.

"One morning when Daddy walked downtown to open up as usual he found the Café's big glass windows smashed to smithereens. [Kristallnacht: not only for Berlin Jews.] He telephoned a repair man. Nobody came. When he finally got the windows replaced, nobody came to eat. He hung on, writing up menus and pasting them on the new windows. No use. So Daddy went away to Merrill to be head chef at the Hotel."

Merrill is a small town twenty miles north of Wausau, far enough by train that my grandfather can't come home weekends when the restaurant is busiest. He sends Emma his laundry in a brown canvas bag with straps.

"Is there something for me?" I pester. And sometimes there is: tucked among union suits, a Mars Bar or better a BLT wrapped in wax paper labeled "Margo." Proust had his madeleines, I have bacon, lettuce, tomato and mayo between slices of Wonder Bread that evoke my whole childhood. Grandfather was thinking of me!

So my grandfather, John Merkel, left Wausau to be head chef at the Hotel Merrill because Germany haters (Wausau is heavily German) smashed his cafe windows. Later my grandfather took a job at the Hotel Manitowoc in eastern Wisconsin, much farther away. No more brown canvas bags with straps. He disappeared. Only now do I realize that his faithful paychecks kept our chins above water.

But Detective Margo, on the trail like Judy Bolton, questions whether it's only the Crystal Cafe disaster that parts my grandparents for long stretches at a time.

My grandfather's carrying a pan of steaming shaving water upstairs to the only bathroom. Emma surges after him. She's sweating, though it's winter. When I shove past him, he lowers his eyes.

No place to hide from Emma, *ever*. I grab a coat and run outside. From the alley the city plow has shifted drifts of snow into the yard. I fling myself into one. Funny, snow sometimes makes you warm. It's one of my puzzles. I'm feeing bad, I think I must have hurt Grandfather's feelings on the stairs. But I don't understand: why he can't shut her mouth? He's her husband, isn't he? Does she hate him because we're poor?

Poor. Always always scraping for quarters, dimes, pennies. Kids, raw fists jammed into pockets, waiting for Central School doors to open, jeer at Mother and me when we pull up in a taxi. They can't know that at twenty-below-zero we can scrape together a quarter for a cab but not one dollar toward a car. We can't even drive. Not Grandfather, not Emma, not Mother, not Aunt Marie. Only Uncle Johnny.

Once, after school, I'm inspired to visit my Great Grandmother Wilhelmina Klade on Forest Street. At eighty she is a beautiful woman with high cheekbones, few wrinkles, and an air of aristocratic calm. She is rocking, hands looping wool over needles into a scarf. In my whole life I've exchanged twenty words with her. We have an uneasy chat, but as I leave she reaches for her purse, probes it, and gives me a penny. I am dazzled. Next day I return: another chat, another penny. I've struck a gold mine. On my fifth visit she looks at me sadly. "You don't come for me, Margo, you come for my pennies."

I think Emma worked at the Crystal Cafe until children began to be born in 1908: Marie, then John, then my mother, Elsie Juanita, Juanita after a currently popular song.

"I wasn't wanted," Mother announces out of nowhere. I'd met her after work and we'd toiled up steep Scott Street to Stewart's Park, gift of the wealthy family who lives just across the street in a mansion behind tall walls. We're perched on the edge of the goldfish pond with its plashing fountain. I *love that fountain*. Somber under black branches of pines, the park slopes down to a curved amphitheater against which, Mother tells me, young women used to dance at dusk in white gauze, like moths.

I love my park.

Mother lights a ciggy.

"My parents had their boy and their girl. And Mother, your grandmother, lived in terror of another pregnancy. This she's told me many times."

"She said she didn't want you?"

"Often. Then to make up for telling me plainly I wasn't wanted, she spoiled me. Wouldn't let me cook or sew or do dishes or dust, bought me nicer clothes than Marie's."

I feel so sad I slide my arm around her waist. She gently detaches my arm and returns it.

"I don't like to be touched."

Her skin is opaque, white; I've never seen her tan.

Why didn't Emma want a third child? *Money*—another mouth to feed? My only clue.

The emotions of an only child—no siblings to love, hate, compete for parents' affection, bond with—are sucked like dust into the powerful adult vacuum-cleaner. I am prematurely old. The whispered conversations of Mother and Aunt Marie are as tempting as Oreos before dinner. I home in on them, lusting for a bite.

Mother and Marie are lounging in striped-canvas chairs under Snow and Winesap apple trees on the cement square that might have been a garage. I'm fooling with a croquet ball.

"Sex-starved, that's the problem." Marie's a college dean, maybe deans talk this way. She's unmarried and, as far as I know (*nothing*), a virgin.

"Frustrated," murmurs Mother. She drags at her Pall Mall then flips her wrist under the chair in case Emma's spying at the kitchen window.

The new orange and green-striped lawn chairs are courtesy of Marie, the only family member who seems to have a dime. There never was money for a garage, let alone a car, so Marie set pots of geraniums around the edge and christened the cement "The Patio."

"Did it begin with Daddy going to Merrill?"

"I think so. His kitchen had big walk-in freezers—you know: hot kitchen, then the freezer to get his chickens and beef. It weakened his system."

"How weakened?"

The back of the canvas chair lifts as Marie shrugs. "He became deathly ill for half a year. I don't think there was sex after that, Sis. I think Dad became impotent."

I don't know what *impotent* means but I smack the croquet ball so hard it flies into the alley. I run after it, chasing my thoughts. After Mother's birth, Emma lived in terror of a fourth pregnancy: Mother's words. Yet she wanted sex? Too much for me. I kind of know about pregnancy, I don't get sex. I just seem cursed to remember every word I hear.

After their deaths I find letters my grandparents exchanged those years of his exile. He left Wausau to get away from her; she hated him, right? (*You call yourself a MAN?*)

John to Emma: *"I roasted fifteen chickens for Sunday dinner, ran out, and folks had to content themselves with turkey and gravy. Rheumatism pretty bad in my left shoulder, I'm rubbing it with Ben Gay as you direct. This evening I walked miles, finding streets in Merrill I never knew existed."*

Emma to John: "*I scraped enough together to pay the coal bill but heaven only knows where money for Margo's new shoes is going to come from. The Salvation Army was here today collecting and I was ashamed I had only two dimes to give. . . . Now, John, take care of yourself, my dear, and wrap your neck nights with hot flannel, that soothes the ache.*"

"*Thank you, dearest Emma for the box of lineament and the oranges. I ate one tonight and it was good and sweet.*"

These yellowed letters, written elegantly in black ink, unveiled a mystery I didn't know I had to solve. A contemptuous wife and an absent husband may have loved each other.

CHAPTER SIX

The house I grew up in was "mean." Yes, my grandparents had little money, but poverty alone doesn't doom a house. True, our lot *seemed* narrower compared to the spacious acre below with its shady yard, big clapboard house and long porch. Across the street a three-storied Victorian castle didn't help our image.

Summers I play jacks on our front walk. It's always crawling with ants. Our front porch is stuffed with old wicker that Aunt Marie valiantly repaints every summer. In winter the front door's protected by a storm door heavy as a safe. When I wrest it open I step directly into the parlor. No entry hall, no coat closet, no place to wipe boots: no prelude. The room is strangely empty. What did Emma mean it to be? It's one of my mysteries.

The family entertainment center, a Philco radio, sits on a table between the two windows through which Emma gazes angrily out at the world from her Windsor chair. The only interesting piece of furniture is a desk with cubbyholes. On it stands a telephone like a black daffodil. A receiver hangs from double prongs. Our number is 9634. I'm forbidden to make calls and only get to speak into the flared mouthpiece when Aunt Marie or Uncle John phone long-distance. They always shout.

Mud-colored carpets try to hide dilapidated oak floors. We have no vacuum. Every spring, Grandfather hauls rugs to the back yard clothesline and attacks them with a looped-iron carpet-beater. His strangled coughs ricochet about the neighborhood. Always, the house sulks beneath an epidermis of dust. Afternoon sun slanting through unwashed windows forms shafts so solid I'm sure mice can run up and down them at will. For years I think that's what sunlight is—thick slabs of dancing dust.

The house was designed to flow from parlor to living room to dining room to kitchen to parlor. Then came The Depression. To save coal, Emma barricaded the rooms with doors. She varnished them an evil brown. Since she didn't allow the varnish to dry before use, the doors are textured with dust, lint, hair, Emma's face powder. They always stick. We burst, not walk into rooms.

The "living room" was cut deep into the high east bank so that it's dark. I quote "living room" because I never saw the family living in it. In search of light Emma cut open a wall and installed

French doors opening onto the front porch. Unfortunately the thick coats of varnish she applied immediately sealed them. Add to the living-room decor mud-colored rugs.

In winter Mother and I huddle at a round table near the only radiator. There's also the Ivors and Pond upright piano at which, according to Ginny Haase, Mother's friends gathered after afternoons of skiing for Emma's chili and hot chocolate and sing-alongs. I am taking piano lessons.

Once I invite a thin, beautiful friend named Carol Jean Streeter to the house.

We sit in the living room on the liver-colored couch. I show her my movie magazines. She shoves them aside, taking in yellowed curtains, dusty carpet, the old upright. For the first time in my life I see a lip curl. "How can you talk about *glamour* in a place like this!" Rejecting the applesauce over stale cornbread that Emma hands round the dining room door, she's gone. I never dare ask her back.

I scorn the room too, except for the piano on which, I'm told, I pick out notes as soon as I can reach the keys—"Just like Mozart." On fire, Mother ships me off to lessons when I'm five to a stern, dark piano genius with a five-o'clock shadow. Mr. Hess so paralyzes me I cannot play a note. Comfortable widows follow, who arch my fingers over the keys and beat to a metronome. The minute they announce a recital I quit. I am not Mozart.

I learn to read notes, I can play pop favorites like "Now Is the Hour" and "Dance, Ballerina, Dance." Sometimes I play from Emma's old music books and she slides into the room, sinks into a chair, and sings "I Dreamed I Dwelt in Marble Halls" in a true contralto.

One day in the piano bench I discover three pieces of music: "Oh, Promise Me," "Liebestraum," and "The Bells of Saint Mary's"—each dashingly signed "Edgar John McCullough." *My father's.* I lick my forefinger to test if the black ink is real, then sneak his music, run upstairs, and hide it in my trunk. Nobody seems to miss it. But my father sang and played those songs. *I have something of his.*

For me, Emma's house is "mean" in a more sinister sense. I still wake, heart pounding, from the dream. I'm playing jacks, the sun's shining, the sidewalk burns my bare legs, bees buzz in the snowball bushes. Then the sun starts dropping behind the trees. I become aware that something behind my back has changed. I scramble to my feet. It's the house. Its eyes have drooped to half-lids, its door is a fanged mouth. It shimmers evil. I whirl round, I will run to the neighbors. But one by one their lights wink out. There is no help anywhere. Only the house, waiting.

Today, braking at the curb in front of 1016 Washington, I'm first struck by the red geraniums rioting over the porch. I can see that Emma's and John's narrow bedroom windows have been replaced by a tall glass arch. The paint's new, so's the roof. I turn my wheels into the curb, set "the Washington Hill" brake. The past sweeps over me. The sidewalk Aunt Hattie tripped swiftly down, followed by Emma's curses. The front walk where I played Jacks until the sun went down. The porch steps we kids clambered up and down, Uncle John making us guess the hand with the stone. I brush wrinkles out of my skirt, run my hands through my hair.

Still no door bell. When no one answers my knock, I walk up the drive.

Still no garage, but someone's transformed the back yard into inviting lawns and gardens. I mount the back steps. Emma, always at the back door.

Instead a young man answers.

"Excuse me for trespassing. I was born and grew up in this house—"

"Come see what my wife and I have done with it."

The kitchen, Emma's filthy lair—unwashed dishes, crusted stove, floor tacky with spilt orange juice, sugar, molasses. Now I see a pleasant sunny room with walnut cabinets, an island with built-in stove and sink, copper-bottom pans gleaming on a rack, fruit bowl on a breakfast table under the windows. Plants. Sunny. *Clean.*

I am dazed. "I recognize nothing."

"We've made lots of changes. Let me show you the rest of the house."

Those dreadful doors gone, the house now flows from kitchen to dining to living to front room. I have to catch my breath. Emma's parlor has turned into a solarium ablaze with green plants.

Casual chairs and a glass coffee table surround a plashing fountain. Unrecognizable, again.

Upstairs the bathroom is sleek with tile, mirrors, chrome, Mother's and my bedrooms bright with fragrant comforters and heaps of pillows. The front bedroom, scene of Emma and John's unimaginable couplings and battles, is serene, lit by the large window I'd seen from the street.

"You must love the house."

"We do."

Until this moment I never realized how much Emma hated it.

CHAPTER SEVEN

It may be the same March I had chicken-pox, or the year after. I'm squatting at the curb poking chunks of snow with a stick into the stream of water braiding itself down the gutter of the steep hill. Aunt Hattie approaches, pauses, throws a nervous glance over her shoulder. Actually, Hattie's pretty brave. Her children cross the street to pass 1016. They call Emma "The Witch."

"Margo, what are you doing? You look awfully cold and wet."

"I'm helping spring come."

I really do feel I'm helping.

The next day Emma forces me into snow pants and sends me off to school. *Nobody* is wearing snow pants in March. The sun having finally made a commitment, girls are running wild in ankle socks. I strip off my pants on Tenth Street, bundle them under my arm, stuff them when I arrive into the cloak room. After school I drop off my friend Mary Jane Hovden at her house at 412 La Salle, then cut up the hill. My thighs and knees burn red with cold under my short plaid skirt, but I love it. The sky is high and round as a blue bowl. Everywhere dirty snow is retreating from straw-colored lawns spiked with blades green as Easter basket grass. Water's shimmying down East Hill, laughing into gutters. I smell earth, I smell sun, I'm high as a kite with a broken string.

On Tenth I pull on my snow pants again. 1016 is pitch quiet when I come in. Emma is nowhere in sight. I distrust a quiet house.

Mother's sitting on my bed. She grimaces, then immediately dimples at me comfortingly. "Grandmother's got 'em again." She shrugs.

O god. Emma's wrath is eternity. Mother makes it sound like something curable, like measles. It's more like rabies, you can die of it.

"We simply have to ignore her," I say in Aunt Marie's voice. Then I narrow my eyes.

"Why are you home early?"

"A neighbor called me at work."

"Why?"

"A little worried about your grandmother."

She smiles and chucks me under the chin. She's not going to tell me, or why she's in my room.

Funny, I'm not comfortable with Mother in my room. Guess I'm the selfish only child, never having to share. But this room is mine, she does have her own. Never do I guess she might need comforting. I aim the lampshade purposefully at my book. I'm reading *Magic for Marigold* by L.M. Montgomery, who has to be a woman. Please, just let me vanish into Marigold's world. Marigold has two grandmothers who adore her.

My room. But even as I claim my pillow, I know that, though I was born in this bed, it's not really my room. Ghosts of Marie, Johnny and Elsie rustle in the corners: "Why *her*?" they murmur, swinging their racquets, dancing the Charleston, leaping into rumble seats. Their trunks haunt my deep closet. Was this Johnny's room before he left, first to teach in a one-room schoolhouse, then to study theology at Lake Forest Seminary, only to lose his faith? That would make sense, Mother and Marie sharing the blue room. I mark my *Marigold* page and look about my room. It's obviously gone downhill since it's mine. My pink chenille spread has bald patches, cracked linoleum scores the floor.

A few pictures grace the walls, but gee I dislike that goody-two-shoes red-haired girl lifting her fat chin to commune with a robin.

My grandparents' bedroom overlooks Washington Street, where interesting things might happen, like Minnie trying to make it up the hill in her 1939 green Plymouth in January. Mother's room overlooks the back yard and neighboring lawns rising to Jefferson Street.

But, according to Mother, my room is a shrine.

"The day you were born I held you in my arms, gazing at the blossoms out the window. You were born in apple blossom time. Edgar and I didn't want a hospital baby. Ginny's father, Doctor Smith, gave me a gas. I laughed and laughed and when I woke up you were in my arms. May 13 is the luckiest day of my life."

I'd love to believe my birth was the luckiest day of Mother's life. But there are no apple blossoms to be seen from the windows of the middle bedroom, so it's hard.

I'm still reading *Marigold* and Mother's doing something to her nails when we hear rumbling on the landing. The landing is

Emma's favorite place because she can terrorize us whether we're up or down.

"*Bastard breeder. Told Johnny to shoot him on sight but that mama's boy couldn't stop a poodle.*"

"What's it about?" I whisper. "Who'd she tell Johnny to shoot on sight?"

My mother tucks a cotton ball into each of my ears. We pile pillows over our heads, we hang on for dear life.

I try to think about Marigold. Marigold is an only child without a father, like me. She lives at Cloud of Spruce with her mother, Young Grandmother, Old Grandmother, and an uncle. She has a pretend friend, Sylvia. My dolls are kind of pretend friends, otherwise I don't have one. My favorite doll is Sonja Heine, she comes with ice skates and skis. But I love them all. Every morning, I dress them for work. "Have a good day at the office," I tell them before I leave for school. Not Tiny Tears, of course, who's wrapped in a pink blanket in a cradle with a music box that plays "Rock-a-Bye Baby" when I want it to.

I can't concentrate. I yank the cotton out of my ears. "*Who did she ask Johnny to shoot on sight?*"

"Ssshhhh." Mother's finger's to her lip as though *we're* the ones rattling windows. "And it's "*Whom did she ask Johnny to shoot.*"

Eventually Emma's on the stairs. My heart's flopping like a netted fish, what if she bursts in on us—a thing too horrible to contemplate! But she doesn't, she slams her bedroom door so hard the whole second floor vibrates. Gradually quiet sifts down over the house. Mother unplugs her cotton ears. We sit up, test the floor with our feet.

It's going on eight o'clock. We're starving.

We tiptoe downstairs. Liberation's in the air. Suddenly I feel what it might be like to live in a home not my grandmother's. We enter her den. A small lamp glows on the kitchen table.

It cannot obscure Emma's counters—garbage dumps of stale bread, unwashed dishes, festering Campbell's soup cans, fruit flies in love with black bananas. And the kitchen floor, I've never seen her scrub the kitchen floor. She flings down a wet rag and shoves it around with her foot.

But, "Meatloaf!" We douse the brick with catsup, saw it to pieces, wolf it down.

Full but wary, we creep upstairs.

"Good night, Miggles. Sleep well."

But I follow her into her room and shut the door behind me. She disappears into her closet, emerges in a blue nightgown, sits at her dressing table to cream her face. I take a deep breath.

"Last summer at the Fair . . ."

She's tissuing off cream in brisk upward strokes so she won't drag down her skin.

"Last summer at the Fair, yes?"

"Grandmother and I were going to see the pigs and sheep in the Ex—"

"Exposition Building?"

"Yes. And suddenly Grandmother yanked my arm."

She stops checking for wrinkles in her mirror. "Why?"

" There was a man and two ladies walking towards us, the man was tall with black hair. He was all in white—"

"What did he do?"

"He stopped."

"And Grandmother?"

"She yanked me away, she hurt my arm. And I couldn't go on any more rides or see the pigs. Who was that man, do you know?"

"I wasn't there, was I." She sighs, tossing the tissues into the wastebasket. "Likely it was your father."

"*My father*?" My father's name is never spoken. Emma, panting: *"That was the devil!"*

"Does he live in Wausau?" My nose has started to sting, I'm going to cry.

"No. But he can come back to Wausau if he wants."

"But why—"

She shakes her head. "Way past bedtime, Miggles, you won't be able to keep your eyes open in school tomorrow. We'll talk about it some other time. Promise."

CHAPTER EIGHT

Emma's house is different when Aunt Marie and Uncle Johnny come home. Though in different ways.

Marie arrives in a rush on the sleek orange and maroon Hiawatha that brakes at the Wausau depot made famous by Employers Mutual Insurance Company ads. Waiting on the brick apron, I clutch a wilting bouquet hastily snatched from Emma's garden. A Negro (we do not know the terms African American or Black) in a white jacket and black trousers with gold stripes swings off the train before it stops and runs ahead to position a step-stool. The conductor in uniform solemnly descends that step and offers his hand to assist the ladies.

Marie wears a grey summer suit over a white blouse, and low black heels. She is tall and slender, the opposite of my mother, who is five-four with a big bosom and round white arms with dimpled elbows. Marie has a high white forehead just bursting with brains and dark wavy hair just touching her shoulders. Her grey-blue eyes assess me, her small mouth smiles. She's not exactly pretty. As a teenager she broke her nose sledding. and since there wasn't money to fix it, there's a bump in the middle.

If she's home for a weekend, we'll walk from the depot up to 1016, I begging to carry her suitcase, then begging her to take it after a block. If she's home for the summer with three suitcases, she pays for a taxi.

By heart I know Emma's first words when she greets her elder daughter. "Marie, you look peaked. You're not eating enough, you need a good long rest."

Rest is what Aunt Marie is not about. Though I hugged her hard at the depot, I know my summer is doomed. No more sneaking out while Emma naps to play street games or meet Helen in the apple orchard at the top of the hill. No more reading *Little Women*, *The Secret Garden* or *The Riddle of the Double Ring* in the new lawn chair with the big green canopy and cushions that stick to the backs of my thighs. Marie paid fifty-two dollars for that chair, the only classy piece of furniture we have. She never relaxes long enough to use it herself.

The second day she's home, I slip out to the front porch, craftily turn the chair so its back is to the front door, pull knees to chin, flip down the canopy. Invisible! Hard to read a book two inches from nose, but safe. Seconds later Marie throws back the canopy leaving me naked as a dug-up worm.

"There you are, Margo! Have you written your birthday thank-yous? High time you learn to iron. I bought an extra brush so you can help paint wicker. The bookshelves in the dining room need dusting. Grandmother wants you to go to the store. I'm tackling the mess in your mother's closet and can use a hand. The patio needs sweeping." Every morning she bursts into my bedroom, yanking up window shades, caroling, "Let us now be up and doing, with a will for any fate. Still achieving, still pursuing, Learn to labor and to wait."

I could throttle whoever wrote that.

We never entertain except when Marie's home. Then she and Mother give the occasional tea party on the lawn, but inside if the weather's cool. Marie digs out old linens, tries to revive them on the ironing board; sets the round table in the living room; runs her new Bissell over the old rugs; arranges flowers in vases. Emma insists on making the refreshments. Pitcher of lemonade, of course, or hot Lipton tea. Lemon jello stuffed with celery and olives on iceberg lettuce with dill pickles.

"Mother, *nobody* serves pickles with jello! And don't I smell the rolls burning?"

Though it's her friends Marie invites, Mother does nothing much to prepare for these parties. Alice Brown Walterbach, Hooky (my kindergarten teacher), Ginny Smith Haase. Mother's old high school crowd.

Emma's been raving all morning so that by now they're spilling tea on freshly laundered cloths, ripping sandwich bread with butter Marie's forgotten to take out of the ice box.

I don't join them, but from the top step I hear everything.

The ladies chat among themselves about curtains (always curtains, why not sheets, table clothes?), a new no-fail fudge recipe, the glads they're raising for the Kiwanis flower show. I writhe because Aunt Marie and Mother have nothing to contribute though Marie's voice is nervously insistent. O god, why do they talk so much: once they start, nobody else can get a word in. Just occasionally there's a bit laughter from the guests and the sound of forks picking cautiously at what's being served. Suddenly Mother exclaims in her thrilling actress voice, "*Just look at the sunlight on those trees!*" I know exactly the painting she's pointing on the wall. "They're on fire!"

Silence.

"Did I tell you Ruth's expecting again?" says Alice briskly. "Her fifth!"

Eventually, Ginny: "I'd like to say hello to Mrs. Merkel. Won't she come out?"

"Mother?" Marie calls in her "special" voice which means *Please don't create a scene.* "Some friends want to say hello."

Eventually I hear Emma's "company" contralto purring smooth and cultivated. I know she's peeking round the doors that separate dining from living room. She never shows herself fully. When the milkman or the paper boy collect, she gives me nickels from a jelly jar to pay them off; if she's forced into a room she snatches up an apron to hold in front of her. She's ashamed of her stomach, she's in mourning for Emma Merkel, 1905.

Aunt Marie's a slave-driver. Second, she's a compulsive talker—like Emma's sister, little black-eyed Ida, who whirrs nonstop while jabbing your ribs in the back seat of the Chevy with an elbow filed to a point. Marie doesn't jab, but: "Don't ask Marie anything," goes the saying, "unless you want to be answered *at length.*"

We're rocking on the porch. Sparrows are quarreling in the arbor vitae hedge. Gee, I'd love to hear what they're saying.

"The Dean threw a gorgeous pot-luck at her lakeshore home before we broke for summer. Wine, of course, and anything else under the good sun you wanted to drink. German potato salad, mustard potato salad, scalloped potatoes, Spanish rice with bacon and chopped green peppers, green bean and onion-ring casserole with crumb crust, baked beans, baked ham, roast chicken, pulled-pork barbecue on home-made buns, Swedish meatballs in cream gravy, lemon jello salad—*real* mayonnaise—avocados with French dressing, tomatoes with thinly-sliced sweet onion—"

Marie gray eyes are locked on the post in front of her, she's in a word-trance. Marie, Johnny and Elsie don't look at people when they talk. Is it because they don't want to see their victims writhe? They're addicted to words but don't dare lock eyes with their audience. Even my quiet mother can get up steam, preventing interruptions by drawling "And then . . . and then . . . and then . . ."

"—And for dessert lemon meringue pie, rhubarb pie with custard, German chocolate—"

It's hot. The sparrows are quarreling. I've got nobody to run around with. I stick my fingers in my ears, fill my lungs, and *scream.*

"I miss you always," Emma once wrote Marie, "because you are the only child of mine who likes to talk."

I love "Aunt Rie," but as I get to be eleven, then twelve, she and I really begin to clash.

My very favorite summer outing is to air-conditioned Gruetts Drug Store, where I buy a comic book and climb onto a stool at the marble counter to sip a chocolate soda and devour the latest *Bat Man.*

About four p.m. I get the uneasy feeling I might be missed at home.

Marie's on the front porch painting (yes) wicker. She lays down her paint brush.

"What are you doing with that garbage!" She lunges for my comics.

"Hands off!"

"I won't allow you to bring that trash into the house."

Our eyes lock; I look away. It's because she's always painting or sweeping, it gives her a moral edge. And she's my aunt.

"I'll get rid of them myself," I mutter and bang into the house.

After supper I sneak to the Peterson house below, the one with the soft-maple tree and chickens. I ask for Virginia, who's older than me and really nice. I hand her a big stack of comics.

"Promise you'll let me read them at your house? Promise you'll give them back whenever I want?"

The rest of the summer I devour *Wonder Woman, Green Hornet, Captain America* and *Batman* in her attic, sweat stinging my eyes and trickling into my ears. Then Virginia suddenly moves away. My comics go with her.

Mother belongs to The Book of the Month Club. I open her packages, she doesn't mind. I learn fast that if authors have anything to say about sex they stick it at the end of chapters. Eagerly I comb last paragraphs of *The Foxes of Harrow, Forever Amber* and *Leave Her to Heaven.* The best place for these adventures is that lawn chair with the long green canopy hung with white tassels—though you'd think by now I'd have learned my lesson. I lower my roof, its shade impenetrable except for a slat of sunlight between chair back and canopy. I hold up my hand against the narrow blaze of light and see the blood pink in my fingers. I'm real, then, but not so real as Odalie, Amber or Ellen.

Beautiful Ellen, in a white terry-cloth robe and mirror sunglasses, rows a boat into the middle of a cold, deep, lonely Maine lake. She's pretending to coach her husband's crippled young brother Danny to surprise her husband with his progress. Her real intention, however, is to let Danny drown. Will Ellen, *can* Ellen go through with it!

Back flips the canopy; I'm shelled (to change the metaphor) like a nut. Marie rips the book from my hands, marches into the house, returns with matches, yanks the pages apart, and proceeds to burn Ben Ames Williams in the outdoor fireplace. I watch, furious and frightened but increasingly amused as, biting her lips, she strikes through a whole box of matches. *Leave Her to Heaven* may be hot but it won't catch fire. The book smolders for days; finally I see her raking the remains into a dust pan.

Marie loses face, yet for me *Leave Her to Heaven* is a crisis. If Mother doesn't forbid my reading her grown-up books, why does Marie? She's not my mother, what authority does she have? She only comes home Christmas, Easter and summer vacations. Yet I feel her power. She's in constant contact with Mother by letter and phone, monitoring my life. She can steer my future in a way Mother can't if only because she makes more money. One immediate result of the *LHtoH* conflict is that I become more curious about my aunt.

I'm in the bathroom washing my panties with Lux Flakes that promise youth, beauty, marriage and a rich husband. We're supposed to do our wash in the basement, but Emma's zinc-lined tubs, mangles, rollers, and shelves stacked with festering jars of mince meat and dilly beans give me the creeps, as do the thick moist cobwebs that catch at my hair. (Besides, the basement is Emma's hangout. In winter she can be found there night and day hunched in her chair, feeding the furnace coal by coal, flames dancing like devils in her face. So why is our house always freezing? "Your grandmother's always been deathly afraid of chimney fires," says Mother, pressing her goose-bumply flesh hopelessly against a radiator blowing cool air.)

"Why isn't Marie married?" I drop the question like an ice cube into the warm perfumed air.

Mother's drying her hair. I remember brushing it when I was three. She still wears her naturally-curly hair below her shoulders. Isn't she getting too old to be wearing curls? She looks up from under a towel, frowning. "Marie not married? It's—"

"Complicated, I know." I drape my underwear over the bars of a small drying rack. It will not dry by tomorrow morning. Walking to school in winter in damp underwear happens so often I don't think about it. "But why isn't—?"

"Well," says Mother. She turns her eyes to the steamed-up window, as though trying to summon the past. "Marie never, *ever* got over Louis Keller, Johnny's friend from Lake Forest. Johnny introduced Louis to Marie."

"What happened?"

Mother buries her head in her towel.

She avoids big questions, big answers, so that it's only after my aunt's death that I find letters from a student at Lake Forest Academy named Louis, as well as hers to him, obviously returned. Clearly he's in love with her. But halfway through the correspondence, Marie is writing, *"I hope, dear, you aren't getting disgusted with the frequency of my letters."*

But, Marie, he is, he is, I moan. Can't you *hear* him cooling off? You talk too much, write too much. Oh, Marie, make him wait: *torture him.*

"I always find it difficult to write to you," replies Louis, *"and letters are so easily misunderstood that sometimes I think they shouldn't be written."*

O god, I can see the end, I'm writhing in pain for my aunt.

She invites him to her college graduation in Milwaukee. He doesn't come.

"I feel, Louis," she writes, *"that if I had not gone down in your estimation you would have been here today. One moves heaven and earth if he is*

really concerned, you know. And I don't blame you at all. I have not pleased myself either of late. It is perhaps 'woman's instinct' that causes my reaction—but it tells me you no longer consider our relationship worthwhile. Please do me the honor to know I am not seeking your protestations (nor would I accept them). I had come to love you—but this means, I think, that we should not see each other again."

At this point, when Marie is twenty, Emma chooses to write her kindly: *"Elsie is having a wonderful time. She is quite the heart-smasher. Maybe you can take lessons in how to treat young men from her."*

Don't think I don't appreciate Aunt Marie, because I do. When she's home she hauls out the round wicker table from the cellar, scrubs it, and lays it with a bright yellow cloth so that in good weather, under the apple trees, we can eat Spam sandwiches and peaches with skin rough as cats' tongues. She says funny things like "'I see,' said the blind man as he picked up his hammer and saw" and "'It won't be long now,' said the monkey running his tail through the lawnmower." Of Mosinee, the paper mill town downriver: "If you can't spell it, you can smell it."

And though I know Mother envies Marie's good job and Milwaukee apartment (and Marie envies Elsie's pretty face), I'm glad when she comes home so that Mother temporarily has a companion who talks Grown-Up and shares memories. If Grandfather's home, Marie is sweet and playful with him, calls him "Papa" with respect, sits with him—leaping up, of course, to water geraniums or brush a leaf from a step—while he smokes his pipe on the front porch.

(Emma forbids smoking inside. In winter Grandfather invites frostbite as he smokes his last pipe of the day on the porch. More than once he's forgetfully stuck a hot pipe in a trouser pocket so that when he comes in Emma smells burning and charges out of the kitchen to attack him and beat out flames. What Emma would say if she knew he slips up the hill where Hattie lets him smoke his pipe in her warm living room I'd not like to hear.)

And Emma's not as angry when her dutiful elder daughter is home. Oh, she still can rage. Aunt Marie, bursting into my room:

"Quick, Margo, help me close windows so the neighbors can't hear!" But I feel she bears Marie a grudging respect, if only because she left home. When I was three, Marie sailed to Hawaii with a wealthy family named the Morgenthaus, as tutor to their son Lonnie. She *adored* Hawaii:

> *We can sell the Wausau house, Mother and Dad, and take out a mortgage on a delightful bungalow near Waikiki Beach. I have enough to pay your plane fare. I know Dad can get a job cheffing at a Honolulu hotel. And all you and Edgar have to do, Sis, is save for plane fare and have faith in my wonderful plan!*

Marie sends me Hawaiian grass skirts, leis and a ukelele. *I have faith in her plan.* But, see, this is why Emma's respect is only grudging. Because Marie's a family person, ready to transport everybody to Hawaii. Always coming home for vacations. Calling home twice a week. Writing faithfully. Giving up Hawaii after three years. Sure, she's in Milwaukee most of the time, but

Emma's got her on a short leash. Many years later I learn that Marie took over her parents' mortgage, paying it off twenty dollars a month, year after year. Even that doesn't earn her mother's respect.

Emma is on the landing. "You need to get married, that's what ails you. Running in circles like a chicken with its head cut off. Man's what you need, man would settle you down in a hurry, shut your mouth. You bean-pole with St. Vitus' Dance, you pathetic old maid."

CHAPTER NINE

When Johnny comes marching home, Emma digs out a quarter from a coin purse and gives it to Mother for a taxi from the depot. Johnny is Emma's darling—all hers: hazel eyes, strong chin, slender nose, vitality—plus the indisputable advantage of being male. Early on he soaked up her ambitions like a dry sponge. She focused her frustrated desires on turning him into a genteel playboy who could marry the best girl in town. Johnny never played football, only tennis; never went out for basketball, only the dance floor. Early on, she ruined him.

I hear this story when I'm fifteen.

Judge Okoneski has two daughters, Eunice and Vida. They live on East Hill in a house that frowns down on Tenth Street as the Judge frowns down on his courtroom. Vida's crazy about Johnny. One day she gives a fancy luncheon with champagne and shrimp in aspic and place cards on a crystal-loaded table. She sets Johnny's card in the position of honor on her right. Strolling through the dining room before lunch, Johnny spots his card next to Vida. But at the other end of the table is a card bearing the magic name Nancy Leigh Yawkey. Johnny switches his card.

"And he broke Vida's heart," says Mother. She's at her mirror, plucking her gentle brows. Legends of broken hearts run deep in the family. This one I actually believe. Unmarried Vida Okoneski, pretty, soft-spoken and thin, always treats me with the wistful affection she might feel for a girl who could have been her niece.

So Emma trains Johnny to run with the rich kids. As long he can play party boy at high school football games and in-crowd picnics and dances, he does well. Then the rich boys go off to Harvard or Dartmouth or to their fathers' front offices. Johnny's connections get him a job too—at the Mosinee Paper Mills downriver from Wausau at Little Bull Falls, where the Wausau Group has established a sulfate ("Sulfite you like, sulfate you hate!" chants Marie) pulp processing plant.

All he gets out of this temporary blue-collar job is a lifetime supply of Kraft paper. I'm still using it to wrap Christmas presents. When his rich friends come home from college and Johnny joins them on a clothes-buying spree, Emma gives him such a tongue-lashing accompanied by blows that young Elsie sinks into a corner sobbing, "I hate you, Mother, I hate you!"

So Johnny goes East to try his fortune. Newspaper clippings arrive from Washington. Johnny barefoot at a Rehoboth Beach clambake, Johnny in riding duds at a Virginia hunt, Johnny surrounded by beautiful girls at a debutante charity ball. What he actually does for a living, I don't know. Is this the same uncle who attended Lake Forest Theological Seminary? Who taught in a country school? Who can recite Shakespeare, Browning and Tennyson by the hour?

But Johnny's coming home!

On the day I pace the front porch, waiting. I sing:

O, dear, what can the matter be?
O, dear, what can the matter be?
O, dear, what can the matter be?
Johnny's so long at the Fair.

Johnny's *always* so long at the Fair. It's eternity before a robin's-egg-blue Packard convertible, top down, whips into the drive, brakes shrieking. Mr. Close, the mailman, looks over his shoulder. "Breaks squeak, car's on the cheap."

Not his exact words, but I do know he's insinuating that Johnny's car isn't paid for. I hurl the mail into a chair, dash down the steps. I'm on his neck before he can get out of the car. "Johnny, Johnny, take me for a ride!" (And take me to the Fair.)

Grinning, he leaps from the car, whirls me round until my braids fly like birds. He reaches into the back seat and hoists out a leather suitcase embossed with the brass initials TCW. I grab it but it falls at my feet, a dead weight. "Who's TCW?' I pursue him into the house, jumping up and down, lugging a second case; I'm a filing magnetized by his aura. "Tyrone Chauncey Witherwaggons? Tom Cat Wilson? Tell me, Johnny!"

He bursts through the screen door. Emma's at the stove.

"Hello, Best Girl!"

She continues stirring her saucepan, then sets down the spoon, notices her son, and wipes down her hands on the apron straining across her belly. She steps forward majestically to receive his embrace, then steps back and cocks her head.

"Hark, hark, the dogs do bark, the beggars are coming to town! Some in rags and some in tags and some in velvet gowns."

"Velvet gowns" must be a stab at the Packard convertible, or maybe the pink silk tie Johnny can't possibly afford.

"Always the witty one, Mother. What if I have some velvet gowns for you?"

Johnny's second case turns out to be stuffed with lightly-worn rich people's clothes. Mother, Grandmother and I sit on chairs in a circle in the parlor, watching him pull rabbits from his hat. I don't know where he gets such lovely scarves and slips and dresses. Trouble is, they don't fit, he doesn't have a clue about our sizes. I lay aside a red pleated skirt decorated with a white fuzzy poodle. Next, though, he pulls out a shell-shaped dark-green leather jewelry box for me.

"Made in Italy, finest leather. Barbara Stanwyck donated it to the Junior League. I said, 'That's for Margo.'"

I saw Barbara Stanwyck in *The Lady Eve* when I was eight, she was smart, bossy and glam. "*You know her?*"

"Favorite Niece, Johnny knows the stars."

I *love* the jewelry box, but I *hate* being called "Favorite Niece." I'm his *only* niece.

When Johnny comes home, Emma's house relaxes a little. She throws open windows, unlocks side and back doors. Johnny's the Pied Piper. Suddenly every kid in the neighborhood is in our yard. He stakes the badminton net, sets out croquet hoops, manages games of tag and ring-toss, invents a game of who can hit an apple farthest into the alley with a nine iron. He chalks lines on the cement square and lets us advance line by line by acting out his commands. He trundles us in wheelbarrows. He has kids painting foundations in summer, raking leaves in fall, shoveling snow in winter. They seem to love working for Johnny.

"Mother, let's have some lemonade out here!" Seconds later the back door opens and Emma hands him a big cold pitcher. No frogs at the bottom for Johnny. She doesn't burn the sugar cookies and she produces edible potato salad and baked beans for outdoor picnics. Johnny sharpens sticks for roasting wienies and marshmallows in the horseshoe-shaped fireplace he built. Emma pulls her chair to the dining room window and watches us from behind the curtain.

My favorite game of Johnny's can be played any season. We all start out on the bottom front porch step. Johnny has a stone, shuffles it from hand to hand behind his back, thrusts out his fists. If we tap the hand with the stone we get to move up a step. "Up you go, Patrick me hearty. No, Margo baby, you don't move up with Patrick, you guessed wrong. Attaboy, Junior, first to the top." First back down to the bottom step wins! Johnny doles out a nickel or two pieces of clove gum or a Baby Ruth. "Play it again, play it again," we chant. And he does and does.

When Johnny's home I can tease Emma.

"You say bad things, Grandma, but you can't hurt me!"

She snaps me with a kitchen towel.

"Get out, you little snunk!"

Snunk is her blend of *snip* and *skunk*. I like being called a snunk. It means better times. She's laughing.

When Johnny comes home we go places!

First ritual: driving Grandmother to the cemetery. She's already told me to pick peonies and put them in a vase. Johnny escorts her out the side door to the robins'-egg blue Packard convertible with the squealing brakes. Emma insists he raise the top before she installs herself in the passenger seat. She's wearing a white summer hat and white shoes. Her face is still unlined, her arms and legs slender, but her stomach looks like somebody's strapped a barrel round her middle. She buys her clothes from the Lane Bryant catalogue for "generous women," but she's going to run out of sizes if she puts on more weight. Today she has wrapped herself in an enormous black lace shawl.

We drive to the cemetery via Forest Street so that Emma can look at the house where she was born. She shakes her head. "Poor Mother, isn't anybody keeping it up?" We turn into Grand Avenue, graceful elms touching fingertips across the proud street. I know the way because every Memorial Day teachers herd us into the grade school yard, hand out flags, instruct us to march in straight lines down Grand Avenue to the cemetery, and sing in tune when the band plays "America, the Beautiful."

But we're not visiting Emma's parents' graves, they're still living. No, these are the graves of the beloved grandparents who owned the farm where Indians turned up demanding mush, where young Emma drove home cows, where later she snapped Johnny in a new suit and cap driving a tractor, labeling the photo "Gentleman Farmer." Where *"They were good to me."* To find the older graves we drive down narrow and narrower roads to the very back of the cemetery. With every plot the graves sink lower, the pines grow thicker. Finally Johnny jumps out, opens the door for his mother. She shakes her head: she will not leave the car. She hands Johnny the peonies. He approaches the graves, removes his hat, kneels and sets the vase at the base of the simple stones. When he gets in the car, there are tears in his eyes; none in Emma's.

"Home, Mother?"

"Not yet. Drive me past the Winningers. Always like to see the old Winninger place."

The Winninger house is so far south on Grand Avenue it's almost in Schofield: a big white Colonial with tall pillars.

"Turn into the drive," says Emma. She looks at the house for a long moment. Does she remember Charlie Winninger begging, "Come with me to New York."

"It's time to go home."

Johnny always takes his dad fishing. Because he has a dozen other projects, we don't get started until late afternoon. Emma snorts at our rods and bait buckets: "Fishing? You've never caught a fish, John Merkel, and you never will."

Our destination is Lake Wausau, broad shallow waters created by damming the Wisconsin River below Rib Mountain. We rent an old rowboat with creaky oars. Grandpa's wearing his summer straw hat with a black band. Behind rimless spectacles his eyes are very blue. Johnny is bare-headed and tan, shirt sleeves rolled to his elbows. He rows us far across the lake into the shadow of trees. Grandfather strikes a match, puts it to his pipe, makes little puffing noises. Only when the pipe's properly going does he drop a line. Johnny stands up, casts far out. I do not look at the can of writhing pink worms. Hours crawl by. No fish. A speedboat roars too close, scattering ducks. Waves slap our small boat ka-THUNK ka-THUNK. I clutch the sides.

Johnny rows to another spot. We drop line, sit, wait. The sun sets, red as the coal in Grandfather's third pipe; dark leaps out of the shore and mountain, eager to take possession. I should have worn a sweater. Still no fish, but Grandfather doesn't want to quit. I pray he'll catch something just to spite Emma, but all his nibbles get away and he throws back the small stuff.

Johnny's bored. "Have a try, Favorite Niece," he challenges, handing me his pole and baited hook. It's almost dark. Grandfather's hat glimmers white, his pungent pipe smoke doesn't stop mosquitos from biting. The black lake looks cruel and bottomless. We're taking in water, we're going to sink, our bleached bones are going to be found years from now, washed up like trinkets on the shore. I'm opening my mouth to whine *"Please, can't we go home"* when a jerk on my line knocks me to the bottom of the boat. I manage to hold on to the pole. Peering over the edge I see the bobbin disappear.

"Strike!" yells Johnny. "Don't lose him." He grabs the pole and reels furiously. Suddenly out of the black lunges something huge, black, slimy, bug-eyed and dagger-whiskered that lands on top of me. I shriek.

"Bullhead," says Grandfather with interest. "What do you know."

It's after ten before we get home with the catch of the day. The house is lit top to bottom, meaning that Emma's both furious and worried. She's at the back door, her double-barreled shotgun loaded with scorn.

"Empty-handed, I see. As usual."

"Not at all, Mother," says Johnny.

"Big fish, sweet flesh, good eating," says Grandpa with a shy smile. He proudly hands her the pail. Emma stares.

"Go bury whatever that is in the garden," she says when she recovers. "It's not coming into *my* kitchen."

When Johnny comes home we go out to eat. He takes us to places called supper clubs. I *love* the name "supper club," it makes me feel like I belong when I walk in. Our favorite is Whitie's, north of town, across the road from the Wisconsin River. It seems like a long drive to get there. Mother always goes, Marie when she's home, Grandfather seldom, Emma never. Mother has a cocktail. I *love* the names of cocktails, tonight hers is a Rob Roy. Marie insists strenuously that she can manage only a half glass of wine, so the waitress brings another glass for someone to finish the wine she can't drink. Always she drinks the whole glass. Johnny hardly ever drinks, but tonight he orders a Miller High Life. I'm allowed a Coke. Whitie's specialty is deep-fried chicken. We order chicken but Johnny wants a steak. I eat greedily, licking heavenly greasy crumbs off my fingers when nobody's looking.

Johnny flirts mercilessly with the waitress, chats up people he doesn't know at other tables. And he never neglects Marie. "Do you know you never once raised your head while you ate your salad? I want you to lay your fork down between bites, look around the table, make conversation, then pick up your fork and take another small bite." Heads turn, I stare at my plate, I'm dying. "Never wash down your food with gulps of water, Margo. First a sip of water, then a bite of chicken, a bite of potato, then a bite of beans." This is crazy because Johnny was so greedy for his chicken noodle soup that he burned his mouth and yelled "Damn it!" for all to hear. We order dessert and coffee, I have another coke. Johnny discovers he doesn't have enough money in his wallet to pay the bill. Marie digs in her purse. We stroll out into the evening. In spite of (because of) Johnny it's been fun. But I feel let down: it's over.

Westerly a smoky disc of sun drops behind the trees that edge the Wisconsin River. We stand in the parking lot looking a little lost while Johnny fires up the dubious Packard.

"Let's take a little spin in the country." Maybe Johnny too feels a bit let down.

Mother and I climb into the back and Johnny finds a country road. It's a pure June evening. In the east a full moon pins itself to the darkening sky like a big mother-of-pearl button. Barns, silos, fields and fences gild silver as the moon rises. A perfume of new-mown hay drifts into the car, making me ache with longing—for life? for what I don't yet know?

"Slow down, Johnny," cries Marie. Marie loves Burma Shave ads. Painted on spaced boards, they make a jingle. We chant:

> A man   A miss
> A car   A curve
> He kissed the miss
> And missed the curve
> BURMA SHAVE

That ache again. Mother and Marie don't have a man. Johnny doesn't have a miss, that I know of. I don't have anyone of my very own.

In Emma's house we gobble meals terrified by the silence behind the kitchen door.

"You take the plates into Grandmother, Honey," says Mother, setting down her fork and knife with relief.

"*Why me?*"

"Grandmother likes you," explains Marie, patting her mouth with a napkin. I know she's spitting food into it because I do it all the time.

Our plates had better be clean. Ruining food on purpose only infuriates Emma more when what she's cooked is returned untouched. We try. Sometimes, though, we simply can't swallow leathery pork or vegetables reduced to mush. Then I scrape and stack the plates at the table, Mother opens the door, I slip through, rush the plates to the kitchen counter and run.

Emma bursts through the door, hurling rejected food at our heads.

"Filthy ungrateful rotters!"

Whitie's is so special.

Johnny's in my closet pulling treasures from his private chest. Like mine, it has a yellowed tag wired to the handle: "For Fast and Dependable Service Order and Ship by American Railway Express." These trunks were Grandfather's, from Massachusetts.

Johnny pulls out riding boots, tennis rackets, cans of balls, ice skates, jodhpurs, old photo albums. I grab an album.

"Who are these people?"

"Those, Niecey, are the Alexanders."

Again the Alexanders—this time in dusters and goggles, ready to board their automobiles. Six gleaming cars dwarf the lumber baron's family, not to mention servants in white caps hovering on the lawn.

Poor Johnny.

He polishes a boot with his shirt sleeve.

"Eunice is giving you riding lessons."

"No!" I *hate* being pushed onto people, *hate* taking favors. "Anyway, I don't have riding boots."

Johnny pulls off my shoe and slides my foot into a tall bronze boot. "Stand up." He dents the toe with his thumb. "Not bad, Fave Niece. Just wear extra socks."

I'm sitting next to Eunice Okoneski in her convertible (with brakes that don't squeal) on our way to her horse in the country. Eunice is the opposite of Vida: short, vivid, white-blond hair, big laugh. She pulls up to a red barn, switches off the engine, hops out. I stare in awe as, minutes later, she emerges riding the biggest horse I've ever seen. She looks like a peanut up there in the saddle.

"Pay attention, Margo! Tapper's an American Saddlebred with five gaits. I'll demonstrate. First, the walk." This I know. "Now the trot." The blond peanut lifts-sits-lifts in her stirrups, smooth as silk. "Canter!" rocking past me. "Now the rack." Tapper does something stiff with his legs. "Fifth gait, Singlefoot." Totally lost, I manage to see that her horse is doing a complicated dance with its front feet. "Of course, there's the gallop," she says, dropping nimbly from saddle to ground, "but I don't call that a gait. Now it's your turn. Not my Tapper, he's a tad testy. You can ride Molly."

Johnny's sitting with Vida on the Okoneski porch when we return, reeking beautifully of horse. Eunice slaps my riding boots with her crop. "Margo did fine, now buy her some boots that fit, Johnny. And jodhpurs. She can't ride English in blue-jeans."

And then, having allowed me to glimpse a future of glossy horses and jodhpurs, Johnny jumps into the robin's-egg-blue Packard and drives away. Nobody has money for boots or jodhpurs, least of all my uncle; and jolly Eunice Okoneski never mentions riding again.

And, though Emma doesn't rave while Johnny's home, she's been distilling venom into a brew that spews its poison as soon as he vanishes down the hill.

"Good-for-nothing bastard! Not a cent in his pocket. Society suck-up, and what does it get him? Borrowed cars and debts up to his ears. *Marie had to loan him fifty dollars to get back to Washington.* Filthy, rag-peddling Jew. Hooring with women who won't have him, that male slut—"

I shut my bedroom door.

Emma (seated at left) and her sisters
(clockwise from top) Ida, Minnie, Hattie, and Elsie

Top: Margot's grandfather, John Merkel, Sr.,
at the rear entrance of his Crystal Café

Bottom left: Margot's aunt Marie Merkel
Bottom right: Margot's uncle John (Johnny) Merkel

Top: Elsie McCullough with her divorced husband Edgar in Chicago

Bottom: Margot and her mother, Elsie

Margot McCullough, age 19

CHAPTER TEN

What do I know about my father? From his sheet music I know that his name is Edgar John McCullough, information no one else ever bothered to give me. Nor has Mother kept her promise to tell me about the tall man at the Fair. I haven't seen my father since I was three.

I have a few memories.

Somewhere on Wausau's west side I'm toddling toward a verge that plunges like a waterfall to the sidewalk below. Strong hands scoop me to safety. I think they were my father's.

We live in an upstairs apartment on the corner of Stueben and Fifth. Lugging groceries, Mother hauls me wailing up an outside staircase with treads separated by vast, child-eating spaces. She sets the groceries on a white enamel kitchen table that's cold when I touch it. On that table there's a toaster that flops open spilling burnt crumbs, and a pitcher striped yellow, green, red and black.

To help put away groceries, I open a cupboard door. I see a big dark blob of canned spinach.

Mother shrieks. "Eddie, get your gun." I'm hustled from the room.

How can a rat look like canned spinach? Except that right now canned spinach is the most horrible thing in my life.

Sometimes I'm left alone outside to play. "Please take me home with you," I beg any passerby. I follow them but they always turn and wave me back. "What are you thinking, Elsie? Margo must *not* be allowed outside by herself!" Next morning he leaves and I'm out soliciting again.

A third apartment sits on a shady street in Green Bay, across from a park; and now my father becomes a solid presence. In a dark room on an unmade bed he's tossing me at the ceiling. The ceiling rushes toward me, he's laughing I'm screaming. Mother bursts in. My father gives me one more fling for good measure and spills me onto the bed. He and Mother fight.

My father has a bike. I'm perched on the handlebars a mile above the sidewalk. He starts peddling slowly, he's got a hold of my dress, it's going to be okay. His long legs pump fast and faster, suddenly he leans into a curve and I see the ground sideways, like a robin pulling up a worm. I scream and disgrace myself again.

We're driving in downtown Green Bay in a car that smells of new upholstery.

"Want to steer?"

"I think so."

Pulling me onto his lap, he places my hands on the steering wheel. It is smooth, with ridges. He operates the pedals, ramming a floor stick back and forth—"Shifting." We're doing fine until he slams on the brakes. Before my eyes the whole pavement rears up over our heads. Far below, through the widening gap, I see black water. I howl.

None of these adventures end in catastrophe. My father righted his bike, the rearing pavement was only a drawbridge so big boats could navigate the Fox River. Yet each terrified me and each time my father instigated the terror. I think now he must have been a bored young man trying to have some fun with a small daughter. If only I could have entered into the spirit of things.

In 1940s Wausau, a father is a financial and social necessity.

My friend Helen says, "I'll ask my dad," and my heart drops into a hole.

School: "Take this back to your seat, Margo, and fill out the information about your father." I stare at the form. Father's current address, date of birth, occupation, draft status, parents' names.

"I can't." Kids snigger, but that might be a reaction to the crooked part Emma carved down the back of my skull this morning before braiding my hair.

"You may take it home for your mother to fill out."

"She doesn't know either," I whisper.

"Don't be silly!" Teacher shakes her head as though I'm an idiot. "Of course your mother knows."

But I was right. All Mother can add is my father's birthdate and his parents' names.

At a father-daughter banquet I share a friend's dad. He smiles at me absently over chicken a-la-king but doesn't think to applaud as I squirm between tables to the front of the room to accept my birdwatching and crafts badges. A friend's dad just isn't big enough to go around.

But really I don't know the fathers. When I play at friends' houses they're either not at home or ignore me. It's always the mothers—wiping noses, feeding us cookies, waiting at the curb after school, bandaging a bloody knee, handing out balloons at birthday parties, shooing us off a wet kitchen floor. (Not Mother, of course: she has to work.) Yet I realize that everything belongs to the Fathers: houses, furniture, lawn mowers, bank accounts, cash, cars. I also suspect fathers own their wives and children, though I don't know for sure.

Nobody owns me, though.

I don't belong to anyone.

Because Edgar McCullough's name cannot be pronounced in Emma's presence, and because Mother rarely speaks of him, I know nothing about his family until the day Mother and I board the train to Milwaukee to visit Marie. It's a few weeks before Christmas and the train's packed. We lurch through endless cars—and across the noisy jiggling platforms that connect them—before falling into seats opposite a woman in a red hat. Mother jumps up, but the train's full. She has to sit down again.

"Hello, Elsie," says the woman in the red hat, leaning forward to tap her knee. She's dark and thin-faced.

"Margo, this is your Aunt Verna," Mother says reluctantly, "Edgar's sister."

I nod shyly because I know Mother doesn't want us talking to this Aunt Verna.

Aunt Verna lights a cigarette, inhales, blows smoke through her nose. I cough and she apologetically waves it away. She smiles. "I saw you quite often when you were a baby, but you wouldn't remember me. Do you *know* how many cousins you have who are dying to meet you? Your father has two sisters and five brothers and every one of them has children—*your* cousins. Dozens of cousins! Elsie, how can we get Margo together with them?" She leans back in her seat and studies her cigarette. "Or have I said too much?"

The train pulls into a station. Aunt Verna stubs out her cigarette, climbs into the aisle and stands pitching on high heels as she reaches for a piece of luggage in the overhead. Then she bends down and plants a kiss on the part in my hair.

Mother never mentions her again. Or those dozens of cousins.

Sometimes on weekends Mother and I pack a lunch and set out up the hill for Pavy's Woods. Where Washington Street ends we take turns lifting barbed wire so we can squeeze into pasture. That hurdle passed, we run down the field like spring colts. A stream gurgles at the bottom. Suspense! Will it be quiet, grass trailing in the water like long hair? Or will we have to teeter stone to stone, stumbling, water soaking our ankles? It's quiet.

Pavy's Woods, rising steeply to Town Line Road, is honeycombed with small caves, acrid with rotting leaves and logs. Mushrooms and moss green as emeralds cluster at tree roots. In spring white trilliums spangle the woods like stars. Our favorite picnic spot overlooks the stream from a bridge created by a fallen oak. After eating our Spam sandwiches, we feel lazy, so I pick up a stick and draw a circle on the forest floor below. We've been gathering pine cones and compete to see who can toss into the circle most often.

"Eddie and I used to have picnics here," says Mother.

I sit up, instantly alert. My father.

"He'd build a fire and we'd cook potatoes and steaks. Once he went to three farmhouses on Town Line Road trying to get water to sponge strawberry stains off my new dress. Let me show you something."

Tossing away my pine cones, I follow her deeper into the woods. We stop at an oak tree.

"Stand here. Now look, way up."

I can just make out what looks like initials inside a heart.

"EJ, something? Maybe EJM?"

"EMJ LOVES EJM. *Change the name but not the letter, bad luck follows, never better.*"

I don't understand.

"I'm warning you. Never marry a man with the same last initial as yours. Look at ours: Edgar John McCullough and Elsie Juanita Merkel, all three the same We didn't have a chance."

She turns to go. I grab her hand.

"Mother, why did you and my father get divorced, really?"

She escapes my grip. "Your father lost his job in the Depression. Lots of people lost jobs in the Depression. We had no money. I had to take you home to Grandmother's house."

"But my father came too."

"No."

"Why not?"

"No room." She reties the scarf at her neck. "Johnny was still at home."

I don't believe her.

We idle along the stream, it makes the turf smell ferny and sweet. Sometimes I deliberately lose my balance so my foot lands in the cold water.

"He sent for me, you know, when he found a job in Chicago—"

"*Not me?*"

"Of course, you. We were taking the train. But Grandmother, when she saw you in your sailor hat and new shoes lugging your little suitcase toward the front door—your grandmother cried out and fell to the floor with a heart attack."

"A *real* heart attack?"

"Mmm. After that, how could I leave? Daddy was in Merrill, there was nobody else. Eddie waited a long time for me in Chicago. . . . I think he finally met someone. They married and went out West."

Is this the whole story? Of course not. By 1938 my parents were divorced, but in 1943 Detective Margo found a photograph of Mother and my father, dated that same year, taken in a Chicago nightclub. Edgar McCullough wears an Air Force uniform. His handsome face has acquired a vertical groove in each lean cheek. Mother's face is round as a cupcake under a preposterous hat of fluffy white ostrich feathers.

"What about when you met him in Chicago last year?"

She looks at me with a face I seldom see. "I never met your father in Chicago—"

"—But, Mother, there's a photograph and it's dated 1943."

She gathers up our picnic bags, folding them into precise squares. "I didn't meet your father in Chicago in 1943. The date's a mistake."

(Oh, but it isn't).

Is she afraid I'll tell Grandmother she sneaked away to Chicago to meet Edgar? Nuts! As though I'd tell Emma anything.

But now I understand about the bike. I was ten last year and all the kids were racing around on bicycles. I was crazy for a red Schwinn.

"Write your father," said Mother.

See? She's hardly ever *mentioned* him before, let alone urge me to write him. But since she's just seen him and he's probably said, "'How's Margo?" now she says, "Write your father."

With a prized new maroon Parker pen from Aunt Marie, I write a polite letter telling him what heaven it would be to have my first bicycle—and practical too, since I can run family errands. "P.S. I hope you are in fine health."

Weeks later I find an envelope addressed to me in a dashing black script. I run upstairs, flop on my bed, tear it open.

I read, "I see you have already acquired the habits of a grown woman, and that is, wheedling luxuries out of men."

Never, ever, have I asked him for anything.

I curl up, knees to my chin. Mother's sitting on my bed.

"Why did you tell me to write him!"

"Look," she says, opening her envelope, "he's sent ten dollars."

"Big deal! A new Schwinn costs at least twenty-five."

She tries to poke the ten dollar bill into my fist.

"No! I don't want his money!"

But a family down the hill is selling their daughter's old Schwinn for ten dollars. Rusty fender, left grip missing, *and it's not red.* I write a thank-you letter to my father and ride that bike east north south west. But I take no pride in it.

Next year Mother suggests I ask my father for money for the dentist. (I eat a lot of candy.) I slam her door.

Once I ask Mother, "Why did you marry him?"

"Because I loved his name."

CHAPTER ELEVEN

"Oh, the north wind doth blow, and we shall have snow, and what will poor robin do then, poor thing?" Emma is rocking me in her tall wicker chair, she smells sweet, like baby powder. I'm three and sucking my thumb because I'm awfully worried about poor robin. "He'll fly to the barn to keep himself warm, and hide his head under his wing, poor thing." I suck my thumb harder, he's a poor thing.

I *adore* snow. Lucky for me: Wausau gets lots. There's November's first snow that paints windows with sheets of tiny gravel and greases the sidewalks so you can take a run and slide two yards. By the time school's out the sun's spoiled the fun; but it will snow again and again and again.

I wear a wool navy-blue snow suit with a matching helmet that straps under my chin. It makes me look like a slow-learner. After a day of sledding I appear at the side door, clumped with ice balls hood to boots. Emma whacks at me with her broom. "Just mopped these floors, don't you dare come up, take everything off in the basement." My socks and corduroy pants are soaking, but I'm not stripping in *that* dungeon. I undress on the side steps, ball my clothes under my arm, bolt upstairs and drop them wet behind the bathroom hamper for Mother to deal with. (Or not). I rub myself hard with a towel until I'm warm, then I get into pajamas and a robe, though it's only three in the afternoon. "Once in, no out": Emma's rule. Usually I stay out until my eyebrows sprout frost.

When Johnny's home for Christmas he hauls out the old Flexible Flyer from the basement. The house above Emma's has a steep terrace matched by the alley's drop-off. Johnny hunkers down on the sled, sits me between his legs, gathers the reins. After that heart-catching swoop there's no stopping. Car on Tenth, we're dead! Snow tattoos my face, I scream with joy. Approaching the tracks Johnny digs in and stops us with his boots.

Now we've got to lug the sled back up.

Today at the top of the alley boys are shoving and pushing. Junior barges through the crowd, takes a run and belly-whops over the lip, boots flopping over his back because it's his little sister's sled. Goin' like sixty—but oops, Junior hits the Peterson's garbage can. He leaps up, shaking his fist.

Now boys don't take turns any more, just belly-flop down, shooting across Tenth until they're dots in the distance. My turn. I clutch the rope in both mittens. Running behind my sled, Virginia Petersen thrusts me over the drop. Past Junior's garbage can and I'm just going to zip across Tenth when I'm bashed with a huge sled from behind, go sprawling and eat snow. The boy who hit me, his sled's flying solo to the tracks. We begin the trudge up the alley. Like all the kids I'll keep sledding until the moon turns blue and the last dog is hung.

One winter the drifts are over our heads. Us kids walk to school on snow banks four-foot high that somebody's already tramped down a path on. After school Helen and I race to find a yard where we can make angels. We flop on our backs, row arms and legs back and forth, then sink into the peace, breaths rising like frozen smoke. I stare at branches black against a white sky, I *love* trees in winter. Snowflakes bob mid-air as though they've no place to go, crows cruise overhead, yawking. Crows stay all winter, so do starlings and sparrows (birds Emma hates). Snow's melting down my neck, but gosh I hate to leave because I'll spoil my angel when I scramble up. I don't want to spoil my angel.

Cars trying to climb Washington Street spit snow from chain-wrapped tires. Drivers slide backward down the hill, try again. Some make it, some give up, park their cars at Tenth and plod up the hill. Emma's at the window to watch Aunt Minnie crawl past in her Plymouth. If visiting Emma, fine; but if she makes it up the hill to Hattie, Emma slams the phone on her for weeks.

No car, we always walk. Mother comes home looking like a Russian, her squirrel-trimmed hat tall with snow. Winter mornings I collect frozen milk bottles from the porch, shafts of cream shooting three inches above their rims, topped by Steuber's Dairy labels. If Johnny's home, he gets the cream for his oatmeal.

In winter moons are especially beautiful. Moons matter to Emma. She knows their names: Sap Moon, Hunter's Moon, Milk Moon, Thunder Moon, Strawberry Moon, Wolf Moon. She seizes my chin until I have to look into her witchy green and brown and yellow eyes. "You'll meet your lover under the grass moon." The eyes narrow. *"Don't believe him."*

For the new moon she has great tenderness.

'Cradlekin," she croons, pulling back the curtain to peer at the crescent hanging in the west. "Silverkin. Lady's Slipper." She rocks back and forth. I don't know there's something called "new moon madness."

I too love moons. My favorite "Night Before Christmas" line is "The moon on the breast of the new-fallen snow gave a luster of mid-day to objects below." I don't know the French word for moon—*lune.* Translated into English: lunatic, loony. Even if I did know, I'd cling to Emma's passion and my own. Yet I can hear Aunt Minnie's loudly nudged whisper to Aunt Elsie in my presence: "You know insanity skips a generation."

How friendly. They hope I turn out crazy like Emma.

"Margo is absent far too often," complain my grade-school teachers on my report cards.

Sometimes it's because I don't have a scrap of clean underwear to put on. More often it's fevers, sore throats, coughs.

Before leaving for work, Mother lays a hand on my burning forehead. Smothered in quilts, I'm still shaking.

"Be good, Miggy. Don't make Grandmother come up and down stairs all day."

"Will you bring me something?"

"Maybe."

I open a Judy Bolton, but *The Clue in the Patchwork Quilt* falls from my hand. George Washington's up there somewhere in the ceiling along with a capsizing ship and a kind of leaf man that's sometimes a bear, but I can't find any of them right now. Drifting in and out of sleep I hack, wake, sleep again. Eventually Emma brings me a bowl of Campbell's chicken noodle soup with oyster crackers, and a glass of milk on a tray. She bends over and on my forehead lays a hand that's been wrapped around cups of Hills Brothers all morning long.

"Feverish. Had an aspirin?"

"Mother gave me one."

"Miracle." She goes to the window, snaps up the shade, peers out. "Snow coming: six, seven inches, they say. Neighbor's got five-foot icicles hanging off his roof. Those icicles could kill somebody."

Smiling, she snatches up the tray and leaves.

When I next wake my windows rattle in their frames and snow ticks against the panes like a clock. It's going on supper before Mother opens my door. Her arms are full of packages. Forgetting fever and sore throat, I bounce up. She smells of cigarettes and snow. Even her breath is cold.

Bugs Bunny comics! New Crayolas, a *Gulliver's Travels* coloring book (we saw the movie), and a little pin-ball game I discover I can't win because you have to roll round tiny liquid steel balls until you sink every one.

"Supper's rotting on the stove." Emma on the landing. "Your sick child needs nourishment. In case you care."

Night belongs to Emma. Burning and shivering, I fling off quilts.

Emma yanks them back under my chin, punches up my pillows. She forces into my hand a mug so hot I have to switch it back and forth between my palms.

"What *is* it?"

"Hot water, lemon, honey, brandy. Drink it. My mother gave it to us girls."

She's over me, I have to drink. The liquid burns my throat. A second sip is better. With a third a fiery river flashes through my veins.

Into my room Emma hauls a contraption with four metal feet supporting a tall cylinder perforated on the sides and lid. She strikes a match and the cylinder bursts into flame reeking of kerosene. She adjusts the lid's openings. Yellow cats' eyes are magically thrown onto the ceiling.

"Rub this into your throat and chest. Hard."

Ben Gay fumes scorch my nose, hollow out my skull. She's heating a flannel cloth over the cats' eyes, she leans over and wraps my throat with a burning cloth. I yelp.

"Now you'll sleep."

"Don't make the cats' eyes go away, please, Grandmother."

"*Cats' eyes*? But don't worry, you won't be froze tonight."

Winter means Christmas. I've saved enough allowance to buy Mother four embroidered handkerchiefs in a box tied with a blue ribbon at Kresge's Five and Ten. She'll buy my presents for the family, I hope. I know she's bought *my* presents because her closet is off-limits. But most of her shopping she does Christmas Eve after she gets out of work at five. At Vullings Drug Store she snatches up colognes, boxes of Whitman's Sampler, stationery, bath salts and shower soaps on a string. I try to be at the front door to help her smuggle the goods upstairs to her bedroom. She tosses the packages onto the bed, flops into a chair, lights a cigarette, opens a window and blows exhaustion into the cold night. She still has to wrap them.

Pat Ann tells me the Allens are totally prepared. Her family has a gift-wrapping night. Two weeks before Christmas they clear the dining room table, pop corn, make hot chocolate, and sit down to wrap presents together. But how can they wrap presents for each other when they're all there? Another of my puzzles.

Aunt Marie has been home for days. She's ordered a balsam tree "because it smells like heaven." In the front room I struggle to hold the trunk upright in the stand while she rams in screws to secure it. I rub sticky sap into my palms hoping I'll be able to take the tree with me to bed. But it's not quite right. Marie thrusts one dollar bills into my hand and sends me downtown to Kresge's for more lights and more silver rain. It's almost dark when I get back and she utters a swear word as she tries adding additional lights to the tree. I recklessly toss on silver rain and am rewarded when she takes off her apron, goes to the kitchen and unearths the chunky ruby-red Christmas glasses I love because they turn milk pink.

"Very likely poor Papa will be stuck in Merrill tonight roasting turkeys, but I bought a bottle of his Mogen David in case he gets home."

I guess I hope Grandfather will be home. I flop on the living room couch and shake my favorite snow globe, wishing I could shrink like Alice and slip inside its dome to join the lady and gentleman singing under a lamppost, a book of carols in their hands. I shake the globe again and again, mesmerized by snow falling on lamp, top hat, shawl, enfolding the singers, making them safe.

Emma is at the back door to receive the Christmas turkey from the Wausau *Daily Record Herald*. She tips the boy a dime, thumps the bird onto the counter.

"I've got a husband who's a chef. He better get home to roast this bird if he knows what's good for him."

Now I remember that Grandfather only stokes Emma's fury when he *does* come home. I suppose he reminds her that testing the turkey is his yearly solo, though just his mild presence seems to light her fuse.

Johnny always keeps us in suspense, and I imagine the fabulous parties that must detain him in D.C. Strange, though, he often does come home for Christmas. This is one of those years. Johnny phones. He'll arrive on the Hiawatha at 5 p.m. Christmas Eve. Mother offers to meet him at the depot with a taxi after Vullings.

Muttering and banging, Emma has been making mincemeat pies and small ginger balls rolled in powdered sugar called Pfeffernuse that make me cough. She also sets out glass bowls of mint pillows, peanut brittle, raspberry candies with chewy centers, candy canes. But it's not really Christmas without the huge annual bowl of almonds, brazil nuts, hazel nuts and walnuts. Grandfather can crack a walnut clean down the seam and extract perfect halves with a pick. The rest of us litter.

One urgent conversation from the blue bedroom I overhear every Christmas Eve that Johnny comes home.

"Say, Sis, do you have something I can give Margo? Didn't get a chance—"

"Well." Mother sighs. "I suppose you could give her the roller skates she's asked for, or the set of blocks."

"What have you got for Marie?"

I've seen Johnny tear off a gift tag signed "Love to Aunt Minnie from Elsie" and substitute his own "To Wonderful Aunt Minnie from John E." (His second name is Ernest, he likes the play of his nickname and "John E.") Mother allows him to plunder her Christmas shopping and wrappings, all of which she's charged.

Let's say this Christmas Eve Johnny's home but not Grandfather. Emma serves a sketchy supper we dispatch in ten minutes. But she doesn't burst through the door to curse us. Christmas spirit.

Mother, Marie and Johnny have been invited to the Okoneskis' famous Christmas Eve party. Remember Vida, who is still in love with Johnny? He is the reason Mother and Marie are invited. The Okoneskis serve spiked egg nog and champagne and present each guest with a fat Christmas stocking to take home. Mother shows me hers next morning—a luxurious stocking bursting with treasures.

On Christmas Eve Emma and I are alone.

Emma lugs her chair round the Christmas tree, smashing an ornament or two, so she can tune in. I don't remember what we listen to this night. Benny . . . Hope . . . Burns and Allen . . . Bergen and Charlie McCarthy . . . Jessica Dragonette . . . Crosby? I have to wait until Christmas morning for Lionel Barrymore as Scrooge.

I can listen to the radio or go to bed, where I'm lucky to have *Junior Miss* to read. Though I know Sally Benson's book by heart, I *adore* dear chubby Judy Graves and her dear *normal* parents. I *love* the chapter about the Macy's red coat with the fur collar and Judy's too fat for it and Mrs. Graves sighs, "It doesn't fit you, Judy, it's obviously for Lois," and snippy Lois says, "It certainly isn't for *me,* it's the perfect coat for Judy." Snippy Lois can really come through.

Christmas Eve is the loneliest night of the year.

Christmas Day evening we're invited to Forest Street for supper and a gift exchange. Of course Emma never goes. Mother and Marie desperately wrap presents all afternoon.

"Think Aunt Minnie will like bath salts?"

"You gave her bath salts last year."

"Candy?"

"Johnny's giving her the candy, remember? I have books for Jo Ann."

"I *could* give Aunt Elsie the manicure set from my Okoneski stocking."

"Don't, Sis, you really love it."

Mother and Marie will take a taxi. Johnny's going to pull me all the way to Forest Street on the sled. In winter Wausau men wear stadium coats, stadium boots, and caps with lined earflaps that tie under sturdy chins. Johnny wears a navy wool coat.

A snowball moon turns the world blue. Snowbanks glitter under street lights. Johnny knots the sled rope around his waist, like he's a horse, and starts out at a trot. Sled runners screak over the train tracks. "Oh Dasher, on Dancer, on Prancer and Vixen!" I shout, clutching the sled so I don't fall off when Johnny speeds up.

At Forest Street there will be Great-Grandmother Wilhelmina (her husband died some years ago), Great-Aunt Minnie, and Great-Aunt Elsie and her daughter Jo Ann, a year younger than me.

"We must be specially nice to Jo Ann. She doesn't have a father."

Suddenly I feel very disagreeable.

"Why should we? I don't have a father either."

"Everybody's always specially nice to you."

"You like Jo Ann better than me." I gnaw a cold thumb through my mitten.

"Never, Favorite Niece."

Jo Ann's wearing a Santa hat. "Ho, ho," cries Johnny. "If Jo Ann isn't my favorite Santa! Has she got a big kiss under the mistletoe for her Uncle Johnny?" Jo Ann reaches up her thin arms and kisses Johnny on the mouth under the poisonous berries.

I could kill her.

After turkey, ham, dressing, sweet potatoes, homemade pickle relish, hot rolls and apple and pumpkin pies, we gather in the living room round the tall Christmas tree tipped with a glittery star.

Tis the Hour of Jo Ann. She kneels, spreading her velvet skirt around her, selects an opened box from under the tree.

"These beautifully monogramed towels from Winkelman's my mother received from Aunt Minnie." She tips the box right and left so everyone can see. "These lace-trimmed pillowcases are from Aunt Hattie to my mother. These green velvet slippers are my gift from Aunt Minnie."

She's onstage the way I can never ever be. Now they're going to open our gifts. I hug my knees, wishing I were skating with my friend Claire on the Wausau Jail ice rink. What trash we give them, sometimes *used!*

If Jo Ann dares to kiss Johnny again under the mistletoe!

CHAPTER TWELVE

Because of Emma my friends can't come over to play.

"Come to my house after school, okay?"

"Sure."

"My mom says can I come over your place Saturday afternoon."

"Not a good idea, not Saturday, no."

Emma got rid of my second-grade boyfriend Tommy Krueger with one telephone call to his mother. Tommy never came near me again until my senior year in high school, and then because he was dating my best friend.

Across Washington Street, the Kennedy family has moved into a house with a big front lawn. I'm at the Kennedys' all the time. Their house is actually *heated* and has a big carpeted living room with comfy sofas and chairs. Patrick's pretty mother brings us Toll House cookies warm from the oven.

I am in love with Patrick Kennedy.

Patrick has a thick shock of brown hair that flops over his forehead. He has a snub nose and melting brown eyes. He wears V-necked wool sweaters with snow-white collars. He wears tweed knickers and argyle socks.

He likes me.

I love him. Truly. He is the kindest person I know. We walk to school together every day. His sister Maureen is too young to go to school.

On his carpet we construct Tinker Toy oil rigs and skyscrapers. At his kitchen table, on newspapers, we stamp molds of Mickey Mouse and Goofy out of red, yellow and blue modeling clay. On our stomachs on the carpet we play trucks, snarling "Vroom, vroom."

It's not all smooth. Sometimes Patrick won't play fair. "*All right for you,*" I announce, bouncing to my feet, "I'm going home." I stomp across Washington Street, arms crossed over chest. God, how I hate leaving him.

When I'm six, the Kennedys move away. I sit on our front porch steps, hugging my doll, watching men load their furniture into a van. The family knots for a moment on the front lawn, looking about them vaguely as though they're already gone. Will he wave goodbye? He turns, looks at me over his shoulder, waves his hand before jumping into the back seat of his parents' car. It's only one of the saddest days of my life.

Mother is best friends with Alice Brown Walterbach. Why do best friends insist their daughters be best friends? It's one of my puzzles.

Ann *never* eats at our house, but I, an orphan at the Walterbach table, eat at hers two, three days a week. How Alice must pity poor little Margo McCullough, with No Father and What a Grandmother. Alice's husband is never openly hostile, but I feel he just tolerates me. I can hear their conversations. "Mother, (he never calls his wife Alice) why on earth is Elsie's child's here *again*?"

Mr. Walterbach drags a black elevator shoe because his left leg is shorter than his right. Still, he makes enough money to buy his family a house with a huge lawn, on Jefferson, a block above us. As I say, I'm practically a resident.

Sturdy Ann is a year and a half older than I, with warm brown skin and dark hair chopped in straight bangs above a dark frown. One day she has a new toy sailboat, so we go play in Stewart's Park, pausing on the way to pose for photo in front of the Stewart gate. We're grinning, arm in arm, pretending we live there. I still have the photo, but I've scratched out Ann's face.

I scratched her out after The Incident.

Ann's passion for anatomy emerged with her sixth Christmas when she showed me her Nurse Kit bursting with thermometers, salves, bandages and fluorescent pink pills. Since then she's graduated to ever more sophisticated Doctor Kits. Now, one August afternoon, we climb the ladder to her bedroom under the eaves and stand upright (barely). There are twin beds and one tiny low window. The room's so hot I am panting, we seem totally cut off from the world.

We're playing dolls on the twin beds when she says, "Come over to mine."

I obey.

"What do you look like down there?" Her dark hair swings forward; below the straight bangs her eyes focus below my waist.

I don't get it.

"Let's take off our panties."

"Why?"

"C'mon." She steps out of her panties. She's about to yield mine when Milton Walterbach bursts into the room. How could he have dragged that heavy black shoe up that ladder and surprised us? He aims a finger at me. "Get out of my house." His voice is high and strangled. "Corrupting my daughter! Never come back."

That night in my own room I beat my pillow, squirming with shame. "It's not my fault, it's not my fault, she's older, she started it."

Ann and I manage to stay friends, though I look away when she strikes matches and sets ants on fire. But we scream in united joy running through the sprinkler her dad sets up for us on humid July days, and in late August I eat mountains of newly picked, butter-dripping sweet corn at her table. After supper, Bing Crosby croons "Blue Moon" while we play canasta.

There is something I've felt *really* bad about all my life. Because I belong to the YWCA "Y-Teens" and Emma wants me out of her hair, every summer I find myself on a bus being transported to Camp Wakanda on Clear Lake near Tomahawk, Wisconsin. Camp Wakanda has a Visitors Day, Ann shows up.

(Who's brought her?) I greet her like an ice cube, introduce her to no one, leave her on the pier, show off my back stroke. I treat her like *dirt*. Late afternoon I take her out in a row boat. You'd think by now I'd relent. But no: I row silently while she stares into the water, shoulders hunched in misery.

Only now do I realize I was retaliating against the humiliations I felt I suffered at her house as the Fatherless Child of Divorced Elsie with the Insane Grandmother taken in by Kind Alice. Not Ann's fault.

Helen Sobkoviak lives two blocks up East Hill where houses dwindle into bungalows before Washington Street ends at Mother's and my fenced pasture. Helen is thin, she clips her fine blond hair back with a barrette. She has greenish eyes and a wide mouth that splits easily into a grin. She's my only friend who dares enter Emma's house—though if she hears Emma raving, we say good bye and she walks on up the hill.

Our private kingdom is the apple orchard at the top of the hill, a wilderness of twisted branches, tall grass, fruit greening to ripe, fallen apples underfoot. Like Judy Bolton in *The Clue in the*

Hollow Oak, we thrust secret messages into sap-filled holes; in the very depths of the orchard we flatten the grass and set out whatever scraps we've managed to steal from home for a picnic. Planting our backs against tree trunks, hugging knobby knees, we plan our futures. We're going to be Rita Hayworth, Eleanor Roosevelt, Bette Davis, Amelia Earhart. We're going to be famous and do glorious things. Marriage, babies, laundry, husbands—they never enter our heads.

The orchard is also where we get giggly. One day we stuffed the flat fronts of our T-shirts with grass, molded it into boobs, and sashayed up to Helen's house, wriggling our asses. Mrs. Sobkoviak laughed. Police Sergeant Sobkoviak unbuckled his black leather belt to score our behinds. But we were faster.

I love Helen.

When I was a baby my second cousin Pat Ann ventured into Emma's house, bent over my bassinet, said critically: "Tell her to get going."

I finally got going, but getting together with Hattie Allen's youngest daughter is tough.

Sometimes, as I've said, I have enough nerve to sneak up the hill to Pat Ann's house. When Johnny's home she plays croquet in the back yard and the stone game with neighborhood kids. Sometimes after school we meet at Virginia Peterson's house and play in the attic. Pat Ann makes me a *magical* set of paper dolls, so special and treasured I don't play with them.

At Christmas or Easter we meet at the Forest Street house. In the parlor a wood stove glows and good eats overflow a large wicker table around which swarm the relatives: "half-Indian" Aunt Minnie, brisk and down-to-earth. Twitchy, blinking Ida with her somber husband Uncle Paul and daughters Hazel and Polly. Aunt Elsie, dramatic and cold. Sweet Aunt Hattie and her tubercular husband, if he's home from the San, and daughters Marjorie, June, Mary Lou and Pat Ann—but never Jimmy, their handsome son. At these gatherings I follow Pat Ann like a lamb trailing its ewe. We circle the table. Everything she puts on her plate, I put on mine. I spit out an olive, though.

"You don't like olives *now*," says Pat Ann wisely, "but you will when you're older. They're an acquired taste."

She's all of twelve.

"Bedtime, Margo."

"But, Mother, it's *light* out."

"The sun sets late in summer. Good night, Miggles."

Robins are twittering their good-night song that sounds exactly like their rain song. Another day, another worm, cats didn't get us, sleep tight.

But I'm *not* going to bed.

Most kids out after dark are boys, some of the rougher girls. They judge by performance. You a good sport? Keep up with the gang? Share candy, pop, and nickels? Take some roughing up? Don't snitch if Junior breaks a window?

I'm always afraid the boys going corner me, rough me up, yank up my skirt with their grubby paws, pull down my panties. That doesn't stop me from wanting to play.

One night, Junior does nail the Kryshaks' window with his slingshot. We freeze at the crack of shattering glass.

"*Shit!*"

We flee down a field.

At the bottom Junior twists my arm. He has squinty eyes and a nose the rest of his face might one day grown into.

"You'll tell, you're nuts about Val."

"I won't tell *ever*, I swear."

"You lie, you'd lie till your face falls off."

"Do not! Give you a nickel?"

Junior laughs mirthlessly. "Nickel ain't worth shit on a shingle."

Emma does so much better.

Junior shakes me until my head whips. Then he whirls me round, plants a hand between my shoulder blades and shoves me face down into the wet grass.

I survive.

"Red light, green light, I hope to see the ghost tonight!"

"Red Rover, Red Rover, let Margo come over!"

"Bang, bang, you're dead! No, I'm not. Yes, you are."

"Kick the can!"

"Olly olly oxen free!"

Emma leans forward in her Windsor chair.

"In my day, after dark, when there were neither moon nor stars, neighborhood kids gathered in the street to play games. We played "Run, my good sheep, run" and even the boys hollered when the Wolf jumped out from behind a tree—"

I scream.

"Like that," she nods with a satisfied chuckle.

My best friend, though, is Mother.

Our yearly blow-out is the Wisconsin Valley Fair. I call for her after work on Friday, important in a starched cotton dress smelling of hot iron, my hair skinned back in new braids. We take the bus to Marathon Park. In her plastic summer purse my mother clutches the wages that, over the years, the wealthy publisher has leisurely raised from $24 to $28. The bus lets us off a block from the gates. Teetering on white heels, Mother doesn't walks fast enough. I pull her through the crowd streaming toward the gates. She buys twenty-five and fifteen-cent admission tickets.

We're inside!

Cotton candy first, dissolving to pink syrup in our mouths that runs down our chins. Merry-go-round next—five rides in a row—my horse a black stallion with snorting red nostrils and a gold saddle. The Octopus takes off, whirling and whipping our necks until we stagger off. In the bingo tent under the G 5 I win a twenty-pound jar of Hills Brothers coffee.

"I'll hold it for you, lady," says the Bingo man to Mother.

We sashay down the midway. Mother tugs me to the darts tent, her specialty, and zaps three balloons in a row. What to choose from the top shelf? She wants a glittery Kewpie doll with pink feathers, but I get my way and the man with a snake tattoo circling his arm rakes down the spotted leopard.

Tunnel of Love, feeling dumb with *Mother*. Spook House. Ferris wheel. Loop-de-Loop. Calf with Two Heads. Shoot the Ducks. Pitch-the-Baseball. Merry-go-round again.

"I want to see the cows and sheep!"

In the livestock barn we wander through aisles tangy with ammonia, trying to guess why this Jersey cow has been awarded a blue ribbon and her identical neighbor a red. But oh, the piglets' snouts like pink roses. I hang over their pen, drinking in their milky smell, I want to scoop up each one and snuggle it close.

Mother pulls my dress down over my underpants. I think she's bored.

Dilemma: which tent to patronize for supper? High-Lutheran, Low-Lutheran, Catholic, Presbyterian, Kiwanis? Catholics have the best-looking chili dogs, but Grandmother hates Catholics and we tiptoe past, choose the non-denominational Kiwanis tent, hunker down under its awning on low benches at a long table covered with a red-and-white checked oilcloth punctuated by oases of mustard, relish, and catsup. We order root beer and hot dogs.

It's not enough.

"I *shouldn't*," says Mother, 'but a hamburger with fried onions, please."

"Same." The burgers come wrapped in hot greasy wax paper. I switch to Nehi, she to Dr. Pepper.

Shirt sleeves rolled to elbows, a bald man plants his hands on the table and leans over Mother invitingly. "Kiwanis ladies baked a hunderd pies."

"Don't *tell* me!" cries Mother, feigning anguish, and immediately breaks down. "Apple. No—banana cream!"

"Cherry," says I. "No, blueberry. No—lemon meringue!"

Stuffed to the gills, we stagger down the Midway. Dark is nestling into the tops of the tall tall feathery white pines, pitchmen's shouts and the wheeze of the calliope tear the air, Loop-de-Loop and Ferris wheel lights spangle the hot black sky. I inhale the reek of burnt sugar, frying onions, damp sawdust, gasoline. Suddenly a jet of nausea shoots into my throat. We dash for the woods, I bend double again and again. Mother wipes me down with Kleenex. Dust from the Midway hangs like fog among the pines.

Time for the Grandstand Show.

Never mind I've just been sick, I eat my way through two bags of caramel corn while goggling trapeze artists, country-western bands, dancers, stand-up comedians, a rodeo, and the Wausau Ladies Saxophone Band. At eleven the City Band ceremoniously launches into "America the Beautiful." Rockets foosh into the black sky, hang, fizz, bloom into rivers of pink blue and green. A dazzling cascade of Niagara Falls finale brings the crowd to its feet.

Along the midway the shills have upped their pitch. Mother has a last go at the balloons, pops one, I get a celluloid frog. We collect the twenty-pound jar of coffee. It's past midnight. The buses have stopped running.

We can walk three miles, or take a taxi. Mother shakes out her white plastic purse. One nickel. A taxi's twenty-five cents, thirty with tip.

"Well, I don't care," she says, teetering on one shoe as she massages a sore heel. "We're too bushed to walk, we're taking a cab."

"Must have lost a dollar at the Fair," Mother says brightly as the cabbie pulls into the drive. "If you'll wait a minute, sir, I'll be right back with your money."

"Ain't goin' nowhere."

Mother pushes me ahead up the front steps.

"Show Grandmother the coffee. Tell her you won it for her. She'll like that."

Emma is awake in her Windsor chair. She hands Mother two dimes.

"Knew you'd squander your last cent at the Fair."

"But, Mother, it's thirty with tip."

"You tip him, hoor. You know how."

"Run up to bed, honey," says Mother.

I run upstairs to be sick again into the toilet.

But wow! it's been worth it, though Mother hasn't a nickel until next Friday. In the morning—incredible—Emma thanks me for the coffee.

The Wausau, the Hollywood and the Grand. Have I really seen every movie that's come to town since 1938 or does it just feel that way? For ten cents I can be gotten rid of for five hours at a crack: main feature, ads, newsreel, cartoons, B-feature, previews. In heaven, I follow the usher's white beam down the aisle. Sometimes I have an extra dime to buy Jujubes or Junior Mints.

Joan Fontaine dying of a heart attack for love of Charles Boyer in *The Constant Nymph.* Tyrone Power daring flame-haired Maureen O'Hara to "Call me Jamie Boy." Joseph Cotton insane enough to call weird Jennifer Jones "a distant promise of beauty untouched by the world." Dying matador Tyrone Power whispering to Rita Hayworth, "We'll watch our vineyards grow." Roddy MacDowell's "You're my Lassie come home!"

There they were, a million times larger than my pathetic reality. Betty Grable, June Haver, Cary Grant, Katharine Hepburn, Paul Henreid, Gary Cooper, Jean Arthur, Fred Astaire, Ginger Rogers, James Stewart, Greta Garbo, Betty Hutton, Hope and Crosby, Glenn Ford, Judy Garland, John Garfield, Marjorie Main, Shirley Temple, Charles Boyer, James Cagney, Van Heflin, Lana Turner, Barbara Stanwyck, Lizbeth Scott, Randolph Scott, Henry Fonda, Clark Gable.

Bette Davis.

Bette Davis is my idol, the star who acts out my secret desire to inflict the truth of my emotions on others. Bette Davis is power. Bette Davis is trampy. Bette Davis is angry. Bette Davis is brainy. Bette Davis is woman. Any day I'll back Bette against Emma.

Then again, maybe not.

One late afternoon in October 1942, I stagger out of *Cat People,* absolutely the scariest movie I've ever seen. Simone Simone makes Frankenstein and the Wolf Man look like scout leaders. I'm nine years old, I'm alone, it's dark. Seven endless blocks lie between me and the house I equally dread. Wind tosses lights on their wires, flinging shadows up and down the empty street, leaves fly into my face like bats. Behind every tree I'm sure a cat woman waits, unsheathing her claws as she morphs into a panther.

Criss-crossing railroad tracks glint like ice as they curve away into the dark, box cars hulk at the crossings. They say tramps live in box cars, will rob you for a dime; they say a Wausau girl disappeared in a box car and wound up in Chicago throat slit ear to ear.

I open my coin purse and dump seventeen cents onto the tracks. With no money, I'm safe, aren't I? I walk fast with a straight back, looking neither right nor left nor behind, because if I look the tramps will know I'm scared and come after me. Only two blocks to go. I walk lock-kneed up Washington Street in the middle of the road, willing myself not to run. I can make it.

I bolt through the front door.

Emma's sleeping in her chair, her chin on her chest.

It's okay, I'm safe.

As I tiptoe past, she opens one bright cold eye.

Much later I wonder: does Mother scrape up enough money to send me to the movies not to get rid of me, but to save me from Emma?

CHAPTER THIRTEEN

For years our major occupation has been plotting escape from 1016 Washington. Proofreading real estate ads, Mother circles tempting houses and apartments for rent.

"There's an apartment on La Salle that sounds perfect—second floor, two bedrooms, dining room, large living room with fireplace, sunny, quiet street. There's also one on Sixth that sounds okay, but Sixth has a lot of traffic. Then listen to this on Tenth: second floor, *three* bedrooms, modern kitchen with new appliances, living room south exposure."

"We could use the extra bedroom as a guest room! Let's look at them all!"

Sixth Street's an apartment building sandwiched between a real estate office and a tavern.

"Between you and I, let's not even look."

"Between you and *me*. It's close to your school."

"Between you and *me,* I won't be at Central forever."

La Salle is a comfortable house set well-back from the street. "I converted the upstairs into an apartment after Fred passed," the lady explains. "You'll have your own entrance." We follow her upstairs, she throws open a door.

"I'm afraid it's furnished."

"Wonderful," says Mother.

Oh, gee. Cheerful flowered paper in bedrooms, pretty furniture, a real fireplace.

I tug her arm. "We can have birch log fires!"

"Of course, you're responsible for heat, electricity, water."

"Of course," says Mother easily.

"I have to tell you, I've shown it to others."

"Oh, but we're definitely interested. Please take my name. Elsie McCullough. I'm on the staff of the *Record Herald*. This is the number, but I'll call *you*."

On the sidewalk we hug each other.

"Ultra perfecto! I get the bedroom with the roses."

"Good, because I adore the morning glories." Naturally she'd prefer blue.

Tenth Street is also a converted house atop a steep grassy terrace like the one I remember as a toddler. "Parents aren't home," says a teenager who answers the door, "but I'm allowed to show the apartment."

"It's *very* nice," says Mother in a voice that means, "But we've seen better."

"You can call back this evening when my parents are home."

"Thank you, I *will*."

Evening.

"*Are* you going to call the Tenth Street people?"

"I'm terribly tired. Besides, we fell in love with La Salle, didn't we?"

"Oh, *yes*, but how much is it?"

"Fifty-five."

"Can we afford that?"

"Surely. I told you about my raise."

"Please please please call that nice lady back right now."

"Grandmother will hear."

Emma guards the phone as though expecting a call from FDR or the Devil.

"Then call her from work tomorrow, you have to!"

"Absolutely, I will."

I dream about apartments. I want an emerald-green bedroom with blush-pink accents. I'm saving allowance to buy us new placemats at Kresge's. I rehearse, "Come to my house after school and ask your mother if you can stay for supper."

The barrel around Emma's middle has grown bigger. She does not go to doctors, but S.M.B. Smith pays a house call and orders her to Memorial Hospital (she would die before entering St. Mary's). X-rays show a thirty-pound tumor snuggled inside her belly.

"She'll be hospitalized for two weeks."

O joy.

I discover Mother can actually cook! She makes the food I crave: spaghetti, tuna casserole, pot roast, macaroni and cheese.

"How come?" I ask, forking a big bite of buttery mashed potatoes into my mouth.

"Oh," she says gaily, "in high school I belonged to the SFers—Social Friends: Ginny, Hookie, Alice and all. We'd meet at each other's houses and make fudge and apple pies and chili."

"Not at this house!"

"Oh, yes. Your Grandmother would turn over the kitchen to us."

Another glimpse of an Emma I don't know, can't even imagine.

Our first Saturday afternoon alone, Mother ties on an apron with purpose.

"I'm going to make a cake."

She takes out pans and melts dark squares of Baker's chocolate on low heat. Then she gets out the big red bowl and beats up eggs and sugar. She folds in flour, then milk, pours the rich dark devil's food batter into three round tins, and sets them in the oven. Returning the chocolate pan to the gas burner, she melts more hunks of chocolate, blends them with butter, cream and sugar, removes the pan from the stove, and stirs up a fudge filling.

Into an ancient double boiler she separates egg whites, adds sugar and beats up a storm of icing into snowy peaks. The cakes are done! She sets them on racks on the counter. Between each layer she spreads fudge filling, then swaths the glorious three-tiered cake in Seven-Minute Frosting, flipping it artistically into peaks. She tops the masterpiece with curls of bitter-sweet chocolate and toasted almonds. Finally she unties her apron and stands back to admire.

I'm dancing around the cake. "Wow, wow, wow! I can hardly wait."

"I baked it for Alice."

I stare.

"But you said you made it for us!"

"I don't think I did."

"But, Mother—" My dreams are collapsing. " Can I have one piece—just one?"

"That would spoil it."

Slumped on the back steps, I watch her walk up the alley, triumphantly carrying the only cake I've ever desired away from me.

Leaving Memorial Hospital after a visit to Emma, we spot a For Rent sign across Grand Avenue. Grabbing hands, we scuttle across the busy road.

A small red brick house with green shutters, peaked roof, dormer windows: a fairy-tale house! We knock, no answer. We try the door—locked, like all fairy houses. The fenced back has an apple tree and flower beds. I stand on tiptoe to peer through the back door window.

"You should see the darling kitchen! A brick floor and a breakfast booth! Polka-dot curtains!"

"This house is made for us! Write down the phone number in your notebook."

"You'll call as soon as we get home?"

"Definitely."

"We can move while Grandmother's in the hospital! I want to take my desk. It *is* mine, isn't it?"

"Marie gave it to you."

"And my trunk with my books and stuff!"

The next afternoon when I come home from school I find Emma sitting in her Windsor chair. I stare at her, speechless.

"My tumor was benign," she says, enjoying my dismay. "Taxi brought me home." She pats her stomach. "Guess I'll order a new dress or two."

I look at her stomach, it looks the same. Everything *is* the same. All these years, looking at apartments, plotting how we'd manage the move. We'd get Johnny and Marie home to distract Emma and wouldn't need an actual moving van, just a few trips in Johnny's car. All our plans for nothing.

Now she's on the landing, shouting at Mother's closed door. "I know what you've been up to while my back was turned. Think you're leaving tomorrow, don't you. Forgotten Carroll? Think you and Margo can make it on your own, Crazy-Cunt? Not for a month. Not for a day."

Her words ice my spine.

I'm standing on the front porch. Lightening flickers like snakes' tongues over East Hill. Big hot drops explode as they hit the sidewalk. I snuffle the heavy air, inhale the raw smell of earth rising from the lawn. Emma barges out, drops heavily into a wicker chair. She likes rain, as I do.

"Your mother's not all there, you know."

I'm watching the kings' crowns. Usually rain's just rain, but sometimes rain drops are so big they make individual statements.

"Not quite right in the upper story."

"No, I don't know." I turn on her. "And look who's talking!"

Her cane stings my rump as I flee.

What new evil is Emma trying to graft onto my brain?

I know Mother has limited energy. Home from work, she curls up under an afghan on the living room couch, deaf to my "Let's *do* something!" Deaf also to Emma's "You'll have plenty of time to sleep in the grave." She does sometimes spend hours behind the bathroom or dreaming into her mirror. But that doesn't mean she's crazy!

Over the years, a story emerges . . . .

We're walking home from the Grand, we've seen *Now Voyager* and I am *destroyed*. "What we've haht cahn't be destroyt," I declaim. "It's ah victory ovah the dahk." Paul Henreid lights two cigarettes, puts one between my lips. My sophisticated nostrils snort sophisticated smoke. I lay my hand on his arm. "Let's not ahsk for the moon, we have the stahs . . . "

Mother's not with me. "You know why I went to Carroll College, don't you? I chose it because the *great* actor Alfred Lunt went there. I wanted to be an actress, I wanted the moon. After I was a smash in *Merton of the Movies,* my high school drama teacher said, 'We have got to get our little Helen Hayes to Hollywood!' But I didn't want Hollywood, I wanted the stage. So I won a scholarship to Carroll. . . ."

Two days later we have hiked to Pavy's woods. We're eating bologna sandwiches with a special treat, two bottles of Nehi chilling in the stream.

"About Carroll," says Mother unexpectedly. "Though I had a scholarship, I had to work in a restaurant after classes to make ends meet. My sophomore year I was taking five classes and acting in plays, and there was this boy who liked me and wanted to see me after work when I should have been studying."

"You should have repelled him," I say sternly. I love the word *repelled.*

"Yes, well. I was exhausted and then on top of it all I got this awful toothache. Mother told me to take the bus from Waukesha into Milwaukee to have the tooth pulled. I don't remember the dentist's office or the pulling or anything, it's a blank. Afterwards I was found wandering the streets. Finally somebody asked my name and phone number, and called home. Mother took the train to Milwaukee to bring me back. "That's the end of college for you, my fine lah-dee-da."

"Grandmother was *cruel.*" I'm on Mother's side *always.*

"I'll tell you something you must never repeat. Swear?"

"Swear."

"I *only* wanted to act, but Mother wouldn't hear of it. One day, she and Daddy went to Merrill on the train. I felt utterly hopeless. I went into the kitchen, turned on the gas, opened the oven door, got down on my knees, and stuck my head in. I wanted to kill myself."

"Oh, Mummy, no!"

She gently detaches my arms, smiles brightly into my face.

"But I didn't, did I? And how glad I am, because now"—shaking me lightly—"I have *you.*"

Not for one moment do I believe that I make up for her lost acting career.

I'm in Junior High when I think to ask, because she's in *Stunt Night,* a big show parents put on at Central School: "You know what you said about being such a smash in your high school play?"

"Yes?" She's triumphant, sweating in her spangled green and gold costume after singing "When You Wish Upon a Star" from *Pinocchio.*

"Was Grandmother there?"

"Daddy too. Why?"

I slip away from the crowd.

Just possibly I'm figuring out the answer to my darkest mystery:

What happened to the Emma who welcomed Mother's high school friends with chili and gingerbread and sang with them around the piano? What changed her to the Emma I know?

Mother says Emma never wanted her. Now I slant my Judy Bolton magnifying glass to a new angle. Mother also says that Emma spoiled her, never allowing her to cook, sweep a carpet, or soil her hands. Why? Did Emma sense—even more than with her adored Johnny—that Elsie might vindicate Emma the young beauty applauded on Wausau stages? She'd witnessed Mother's triumph in *Merton of the Movies,* heard "We've got to get our little Helen Hayes to Hollywood!"

I think I'm on to something. Emma wanted Mother to have the career she was born to! Yet who destroyed Mother's chances of becoming an actress? *Emma.* "That's the end of college for you, my fine lah-dee-da."

Home for the summer, Marie has me sewing ties onto outdoor chair cushions. But Detective Margo is still on the trail.

"Aunt Marie, did Grandmother *want* Mother to be an actress?"

Marie's sweeping windfalls off the patio. She rests her chin on the broom handle. She's going to say "it's complicated."

"It's complicated. She may have been a bit jealous. Elsie was very, very talented. But yes, I'd say your Grandmother was supportive. Always worried about money, of course."

"Then why did she drag Mother home from Carroll College and tell her she couldn't go back?"

"Sloppy work, Margo. That tie will break first time somebody sits down, so do it again. What do you mean, Elsie couldn't go back to Carroll? Mother and Dad re-mortgaged the house for her junior year tuition. And I was going to help her financially so she wouldn't have to work so many hours outside classes."

I fling down the cushion.

I don't understand. I'm back at Square One. Judy Bolton, can you solve this? Because it's beyond me.

All those hours and days we scouted for a place to live. I was dead serious, but was Mother? Had she swallowed Emma's poison, known in her heart she could never make it on her own? When Mother told me apartments were already rented, houses taken off the market, I believed her. Today I do the math on the La Salle Street apartment. Mother was earning $128 a month. Rent $55; say utilities $20 a month. That would leave us something like $53 to live on. Maybe we couldn't have afforded La Salle, *but we could have afforded something.*

She believed Emma. We never had a chance.

"Meet me after work, Honey," says Mother. Emma's been home from the hospital more than a month. "There's an apartment on Hamilton."

"Sorry. Helen and I are playing bikes after school. I promised."

CHAPTER FOURTEEN

Mother has a boyfriend! She pats little blooms of rouge on her cheeks and charges two new dresses at Heineman's. I catch her smiling at herself as she studies her face in the front room mirror. She's also been going out evenings.

"Alice is having a little canasta party, Mother."

"Alice had a little canasta party two days ago."

"Everybody's crazy about canasta. I'll teach you and Daddy Canasta when he comes home."

"'Course you will, like you'll jump over the moon. You can't boil water and you expect to catch a *man?*"

I'm not sure how I feel about this boyfriend. I know how I felt about the last.

Berton Medary sold life insurance and came Sundays to take Mother and me out for a drive, waiting at the curb in his green Dodge for us to rush out, still in our church clothes, before Emma can stop us. I'd crawl into a back seat that smelled of old upholstery and say hello to the back of his head. He had brown hair cut straight across the back of a short neck flushed because Mother was sitting beside him. He ears stood open like car doors.

Of course I was glad to get away from the house. But we never did anything fun like we do with Johnny. Berton drove *s-l-o-w-l-y*, as if the Dodge might explode if he floored the gas over thirty. We crawled up Rib Mountain, lugged ourselves up the observation tower, looked down at the land Wau saw. We inched toward the Eau Claire Dells where I was never allowed to wade in the foaming rapids like other kids. Crept along Sherman Avenue to Marathon Park, site of the Wisconsin Valley Fair, where he'd throw his coat over a picnic table and hasten to the refreshment stand to buy us one-scoop vanilla ice cream cones. I remember tilting back my head to suck a last drop of ice cream through the cone and finding myself staring at a big fat white cloud loafing across the blue sky.

Berton Medary.

"We have to be grateful to Berton."

"May I ask *why*?"

I knew perfectly well why we had to be grateful, but was feeling kicky and mean. These Sunday drives seemed to go on for years. Once in a while Mother would say coyly, "I can always marry Berton, you know." I'd stick a finger down my throat.

Now Berton's gone and she has a new boyfriend and I'm hanging out in her room. She's doing her nails. She has beautiful hands with fingers that curl like petals. She's shaped her nails with a file, now she's dipping a wood stick into orange oil and pressing back her cuticles so that the half-moons show. She wipes her nails with a cotton ball, unscrews a bottle of Revlon's "Cherries in the Snow." She applies it carefully, three strokes to a nail and flaps her fingers in the air to dry. Then with a stick dipped in Cutex polish-remover she carves a semi-circle from the base of each nail. By now I'm pretty sure she's not going to Alice's old canasta party.

I *hate* her leaving me alone with Emma, yet I want her to have fun. Maybe she could take me with her. Where's she going? Who's the man?

I'm painting my own stubby nails "Cherries in the Snow" when there's a crash below. I rush downstairs but freeze on the landing. Everything is stalled, like the ominous breath I always feel between thunder clap and lightening.

Wearing one of the new flowered dresses, Mother still bends forward, her right hand about to apply lipstick in the front room mirror. Only there is no mirror. Then I see a jar of Emma's applesauce spinning leisurely on the floor.

Emma has thrown it at Mother. If the jar had struck her head, *she could be dead.*

Before I can move, Emma fastens her capable hands around Mother's throat. She whips her head back and forth so hard her dime-store earrings fly across the room.

"Spreading your legs for some man so you can bring home another bastard?"

Emma is stronger than Mother. She slaved for her parents, raised four younger sisters, drove grandparents' cows, bore three children. She has three inches on Mother and lots of heft.

I run to the kitchen, grab Emma's broom, raise it and bring it down on her head—once, twice, thrice. *Do you think we're friends just because you're here when Mother's gone, just because you rock me and sing me old songs, just because you cook my supper?*

But the broom is bewitched and only bounces off her head like a feather-duster. Emma turns and looks at me over her shoulder. Time stops. She studies me as though seeing me for the first time. She registers my anger. She gauges my young strength.

A car honks at the curb. She drops her hands. Mother lurches out the front door.

I run upstairs and throw myself into the heap of old quilts piled in my closet. Emma is going to kill Mother.

Unless I kill Emma first.

Mother's new boyfriend turns out to be an announcer for the local radio station. I first hear John's voice one Sunday morning doing a commercial for Land o' Lakes Bakery. He begins confidently, "For the breast in bed—"

Mother's?

The three-story mansion across from us has been converted into apartments; John, I discover, occupies third floor. His black hair is thinning; he has what Gillette razor ads call "five o'clock shadow." He is good-looking, tall, just the right weight. One summer day I am walking to the Presbyterian Church to teach

Summer Daily Bible School. From across the street I see him and Mother walking together, swinging hands. He's younger than she but you can't tell—much. *She's so happy.* O god, I'm losing her, *I hate him.* She drops his hand, waves to me. I turn coldly away.

Oh, but he's cool. He's *it* in Wausau.

If I save my allowance, I can sometimes eat at Vulling's Drug Store, which serves fabulous ham-salad sandwiches. One day I find myself on a stool next to Mother's boyfriend. It will be the first time we've met. In case he doesn't know I'm Elsie McCullough's daughter, I introduce myself. He's got a terrible cold, inconvenient for Local Radio Star.

"Nice to meet you," he moans. "Always remeber, Mardo: for a code, fried udyons."

Not quite the first conversation with Mother's boyfriend I'd imagined.

CHAPTER FIFTEEN

The upstairs of Emma's house contains four vast, dark closets. The whole house is an unexploded mine, but of the closets I'm especially wary. Off-limits, they are dangerous and unexplained. I imagine that in their bellies lurk the darkest secrets of the house.

Even the mysteries of my own closet I can't solve, though my own big trunk (Grandfather's really, with a Massachusetts shipping label) holds all my treasures: Story Book dolls in their polka-dot boxes; favorite books like the *Raggedy Anns, Magic for Marigold, Bambi, The Dog of Flanders, Treasure Island* and my Judy Boltons. Also my red felt-covered diaries with brass locks and tiny keys; if anybody opened these, I'd die. Some treasures of Johnny's trunk I glimpse when he comes home. A third trunk is severely locked. Marie's.

No light in any closet. Exploring mine, I wedge back the door to the place where it catches the linoleum and shine my Girl Scout flashlight into its entrails. Behind my dreary duds, a mystery rank of fabrics recede into darkness. I touch them reverently as I move along. Beaded dresses, tissuey dresses with uneven hems, slippery negligées. Silk kimonos so thin they shred their silk as I touch them. Satin dance slippers, worn saddle shoes, canvas tennies with knotted laces. I cry out as an animal brushes my cheek, breathe again: only the harmless remains of a fur coat. When could the Merkels have afforded fur coats, I wonder. Perhaps in the hey-day of the Crystal Cafe? The fur coat marks the end of my explorations: beyond, dark sucks away the beam of my flashlight and I retreat.

  Margo, the spoiled only child who's never had to share a bedroom or toys or attention, is forced to admit that life went on abundantly before she existed; a life, moreover, I can never experience or, given the secretive nature of my family, understand. Maybe this is why I've always been in love with the past: out of reach yet desirable and so preferable to my semi-squalid present. Though I consider myself stubborn and self-centered, I hardly feel that I am present in this family—as though my life only takes color from vivid stains of the past.

Whenever she's at work I briskly rummage Mother's closet. *What, I want to know, is a woman?* One day the search ends when I discover a fat red book hidden in a hat box. I rush it to my room. It seems to be about *reproduction*. My eyes bug at the illustrations. I sneak it back onto her closet shelf, but in coming days learn about vaginas, penises, vas deferens, labia, vulvas, scrotums, uteruses, penetration, ejaculation, sperm, eggs, fetuses. I keep returning it to Mother's closet, pages hot and limp.

I'm in seventh grade. My Home Ec partner and I are beating eggs into cake batter when I double over. Teacher tries to straighten me, can't, escorts me, hobbling, to the school nurse who says briskly, "You're probably getting your first period, you're excused to go home." In cruel broad daylight I limp the six blocks to 1016 Washington; when Emma opens the door I manage to look her in the eye.

"What ill wind blows you home?"

"I threw up in Home Ec but I'm fine now."

I know the bottom drawer where Mother's stashed the stuff: Kotex pads, disposable sanitary bags. But no knock-out drops for cramps. I unzip my skirt, step out of my panties. I've heard about *the stain;* I've seen Mother's dark blood smelling like waste; felt its metallic taste on my tongue. Nothing doing with me yet, but I'm dying. Fasten belt around waist, pull napkin from box, clip gauze ends of Kotex pad to belt. Wrap myself in her robe, shut her door and spread a blanket under me before I crawl under her bedspread, not wanting to hemorrhage over the sky blue. Look at the watch Aunt Marie gave me. Two-thirty. An eternity before Mother comes home.

    In Mother's bottom drawer I'd also noticed three flat boxes. Now I crawl off the bed, find and open them. In the first I find dark locks wrapped in green tissue; they must be Marie's. Mother's gold curls coil the second box. Mother and Marie must have had their hair shingled in the Roaring Twenties, taken home what they'd sacrificed.

    In the third box is a certificate. Frowning over the inky handwriting, I decipher that Edgar John McCullough and Elsie Juanita Merkel were united in marriage on October 17, 1932.

    Before devouring Dr. X's red book on reproduction, I'd have tossed the certificate back into the drawer. Now, though, I count nine months backward on my fingers from May 13. I'm rotten at math, but it seems that about August 13, 1932, I was conceived.

Marie: "I don't know where you got the idea your mother couldn't go back to Carroll College. Mother and Dad re-mortgaged the house to pay for her junior year."

Now I understand.

Mother didn't return to Carroll because she'd had a nervous breakdown in Milwaukee—though Emma held that over her for years. Or because there wasn't money. Or because Emma vetoed an acting career.

She didn't return because she was pregnant with me.

Mother makes an entrance smelling of "Emeraude" and Pall Malls and puts on a cheery face. "Congratulations, Miggy, you're a woman now. Nothing abnormal, we've discussed it. Cramps, honey?"

I nod miserably.

"Tell you what, go cuddle in your quilt and I'll bring you up supper."

"Not hungry."

"You will be."

That long evening in bed bestows upon me a gift: answers to questions tormenting me for years. Answers satisfactory, at least, to Detective Margo, twelve years of age.

What changed Emma Merkel from a normal woman into a raging beast?

Her father's fury bit deep into her, for sure. Fierce jealousy of her sister Hattie. Grandfather's impotence, as reported by Mother and Marie. Frustration at being poor.

But also, I feel certain now, the death of her dream that "our little Helen Hayes," might be the star Emma wanted to be herself.

When did she change? It must have been that autumn of 1932 when Mother had to admit she was pregnant.

Why is my father The Devil? Because Emma blames him and him only for ruining her daughter's career. Elsie's divorce confirms he's Satan (though Emma would have loathed more a successful marriage). Emma decrees Edgar McCullough and his kin taboo for the rest of my life.

I am eighteen when I finally see my mother act. She is better than Helen Hayes. She sweeps on as Irina Arkadina, the fading actress in *The Seagull,* and steals the play with her first line. She doesn't seem to be acting, yet I know how expertly she is. In the dark I sob into my hands for her wasted gift.

After her death I find a diary she started when she was nineteen. She was indeed a heart-smasher—dates with Bob, Melvin, Wilbur, Paul, Firpo, Glenn and Eddie McCullough trip over themselves. (I regret Firpo, I would have called him that, like Scout called her father Atticus.) Typical entry: "Paul was coming up when Bob called. Paul got here first and I told him complications had arisen. He left gentlemanly."

Bob, Melvin, Firpo and Co. exit as Eddie McCullough takes center stage as Mother's leading man. From a starred August 11, 1932 entry, I believe I know the date of my conception. "It was fun target-shooting with Eddie in Paff's and romantic watching the fire die. Then *------! 'A log cabin with a stream' etc."

It's midnight before the cramps relent. I check my Kotex pad. It flaunts a crimson sash. So now I am a woman.

I don't feel like a woman. I feel like a spoiler, thinking of the brilliant life Mother—and Emma—could have lived onstage if only it hadn't been for me.

CHAPTER SIXTEEN

Now that I'm thirteen, I dab on lipstick from Mother's tube of Tangee. Ninth-grade girls wear lipstick to school and strands of fake pearls with cashmere sweaters. Seventh-graders like me wear pleated skirts, white blouses with Peter Pan collars, and bobby socks with saddle shoes or penny loafers. We also wear charm bracelets. I have fourteen charms on mine, my favorites are a grand piano and a windmill with arms that really turn. I'm going through a stage Mother assures me is "puppy fat." All I know is that it puts me into a department and a size called "Chubette."

The shame.

Junior High changes my landscape. What has happened to Helen, to Ann Walterbach? John Marshall and St. James's Catholic School sends us its nurslings. From the south side, a talented, excitable girl named Gloria Kannenberg bursts onto the scene and we become friends. One Saturday she calls. Emma answers.

"I know you," says Emma, "Margo's mentioned you. We East Hill people don't associate with West-Siders."

"But my father's a state senator."

"Doesn't matter, Elsie and Margo don't care to make your acquaintance. *Do not call this number again.*"

Against my violent protests, Mother enrolls me in Mrs. Murray's Saturday afternoon YWCA Dancing School. Emma clamps a curling iron on my naturally-curly brown hair until I look like Little Lulu. Under the delusion she can sew, she forces upon me garments fresh from her machine, threads springing from slippery sateen or scratchy wool.

There's a shoe repair shop that I've stopped at since kindergarten because in the window a green parrot sways from foot to foot on its perch, cocking its head amiably at me and rolling its eye. Today I linger, tapping the pane as the minutes tick ruthlessly toward three o'clock. "Don't feel bad," I tell my friend, "I'm trapped just like you."

Mrs. Murray is a middle-aged woman with upswept black hair, a large bosom bespangled with ropes of pearl, and one leg much shorter than the other so that when demonstrating the fox trot or rhumba she lurches like a drunk. Inevitably I end up with some geek, sweaty palms glued together. Once, though, for "String of Pearls" Mrs. Murray pairs me with an East Hill boy. This East Hill boy does not look at me the whole dance. Before the last notes he drops my hand like it's a snake and bolts across the room to his buddies, who surround him sympathetically. Head high, I walk off the floor. In the cloakroom I begin to cry. I don't have a Kleenex so I wipe my nose on a random sleeve, hoping to ruin some East Hill bitch's polo coat.

"Come out, come out, wherever you are!" Mrs. Murray staggers in, blots my tears with a perfumed handkerchief and a smile.

"Never never am I going back in there!"

"Yes, you are, Margo. Your rhumba needs considerably more work."

A boy or two seems to like me. Yet how can I pay attention to them when I have a violent crush on my dark-haired science teacher, Mr. Sleeter? My crush lasts from January to April, when it's bike time again and I peddle to where I know he lives on the

South side. What will I do when I find his house! Knock at his door? Push my love note through his mailbox slot?

It's twilight when I dismount, prop my bike against shrubbery. His house is disappointingly small, the living room lit with a bare bulb hanging from the ceiling. Through the picture window I see Mr. Sleeter on a ladder. He is swigging a can of Blatz and painting a wall. He is wearing shorts and a sleeveless white undershirt. Black hair sprouts like shrubbery from his arm pits. I take in the scene, whip round my bike and peddle home.

Really, I know nothing about men or boys. Think of my family. Emma, one of five girls. Herself the mother of two girls and one boy. Great Aunt Hattie: four girls and a boy. Great Aunt Ida: two girls. Great Aunt Minnie: unmarried. Great Aunt Elsie: one girl. I have no father or brothers. Grandfather is seldom home. I see Johnny sometimes, but Johnny's always Master of Ceremonies. You can worship a Master of Ceremonies, but you can't get really close.

Then there's my father's family, chock-full of uncles and male cousins I'm forbidden to associate with.

So that when I fall violently in love at thirteen, the man is naturally not only unobtainable but an image on a screen. One Saturday in July 1946, swinging my patent-leather purse weighted with a hankie, two barrettes and 40 cents, I breeze downtown to the Grand Theater and thrust my quarter through a plastic tunnel to a woman with dyed black hair and a tired face. A twerp of an usher in a maroon uniform aims his flashlight down the aisle, I follow him. I choose a seat in my favorite fifth row and settle into the expectant dark to munch malted milk balls. The featured movie is a British film I've never heard of called *The Seventh Veil.*

A young girl, Francesca Cunningham, is sent to live with her bachelor cousin, Nicolas. A servant shows her into Nicolas's drawing room. She stands just inside the door in a hat and short coat, clutching a school satchel. The camera pans forward to a man in a dark suit seated in a wing chair reading a newspaper, a Persian cat on his lap. The girl is announced, he lowers his paper and looks round the edge of his chair without curiosity.

Before I even hear the most seductive voice in filmdom, I've fallen in love with James Mason.

Oh, there've been other dark men—Tyrone Power, Cornell Wilde, Laurence Olivier. My absent father. This is different.

I waft up Washington Street in a London fog. James Mason! Suave, detached, ironic eyebrows, kindling dark eyes, flared nostrils, purring, aristocratically-weary voice. I steady myself against the trunk of an elm. *Be still, my heart.*

Borrowing against two months' allowance, I manage to see *The Seventh Veil* once for every veil before it leaves the Grand.

Mother and I are doing dishes. I *have to* pronounce his name.

"Tell me about him," I demand, filing imperfectly dried plates in a cupboard. "Describe him to me."

"Who?" asks Mother absently, lovely manicured hands deep in suds.

"*James*, of course!"

"Well." She hesitates. "He certainly has nice brown eyes."

"*Nice*? They're magnificent, dark and glowing. What else? Do you think he's handsome?"

"I guess so."

"What else?"

"Dark hair. Nice dark hair."

"*Nice* is all you can say? Then what do you think he's *like*?"

"In what way?"

"In every way. Do you think he's kind?"

"He beat Ann Todd with a riding crop. That's horrid."

"Mother, it was a *movie*. Is he intelligent, do you think?"

"Oh, I imagine so." She absently scrubs a frying pan, staring through the cracked wall over the sink into sweeter vistas. "I think he has a very intelligent face."

"Sensitive?"

She smiles dreamily. "Very sensitive."

"Sexy?"

"Very."

"You know his wife, Pamela, is *totally* unworthy. Do you think he'll divorce her if he meets me?"

"I don't know, Honey. How are you going to meet him?"

I ignore the question. "If we married, do you think we'd get along?"

Her head bows lower over the soapsuds.

"Well, *would* we?"

It does not occur to me that, perhaps because my father's hair was black, I am in thrall to dark men. Later that night, sitting cross-legged on my bed, I'm cutting out an article from *Modern Screen* to paste into my fattening JAMES MASON SCRAPBOOK. He's made a sensation in America, I've joined his fan club, I'm furiously borrowing money from Mother to buy movie mags. I squeeze a line of LePage's glue across the top of the page, smooth down the article with a tender hand. Turn the sacred pages slowly.

Then it hits me. Doing dishes, I thought we were talking about *James*. I was, but Mother was talking about John the Radio Announcer. *Traitor.*

We're in her blue bedroom, not winter, not autumn. Spring, maybe June. Mother's birthday is June seventh. I don't remember what we're doing. I'm probably watching her unscrew earrings, kick off shoes, stretch her plump white arms, yawn—become my mother again. Though now she's the brand-new Society Editor of the *Wausau Daily Record-Herald.*

No, she doesn't yawns. She looks at me brightly and says:

"I think you should stop calling me Mother."

I don't remember what I say.

She crosses a leg and begins massaging a stockinged foot. A small run has started above the toe. She grins, leans forward to explain.

"Everyone says we look more like sisters than mother and daughter."

"Who's *everyone*?"

"Oh, Alice, Ginny, Hookie, Irvin Marquart, you know the high school teacher, lives down at the corner. Your *Grandmother*. The other day she said I look like the heart-smasher of old. Actually all my friends, honey—and John. Actually, and this is important, I'd like you to start calling me Elise."

"Elise?"

"Borden's Elsie the Cow ruined my name for me forever." She makes a tragic face and moos.

"I'll never call you Elise."

"Elsie, then."

"But, Mother, calling you Elsie doesn't *feel* right."

"But, Honey, I *want* you to."

We face each other in her bedroom with the blue walls, blue bedspread, blue dressing table, blue rugs. I can't see any options here but "Okay" or "Never."

I walk out, closing the door behind me, I toss on my bed. She's still such a pal, such an ally against Emma. How can I *not* do something so simple for her?

I can't.

I must.

Despair covers me like deep snow.

The next day it hits me: the realization that with those words—"I think you should stop calling me 'Mother'"—*she has orphaned me*. Now I have neither mother nor father.

Wait.

I do have a mother.

We both do.

Her name is Emma Merkel.

CHAPTER SEVENTEEN

I'm fourteen, with a boyfriend or two. Probably they're only interested in the new breasts I try to hide behind my blue ring-binder school notebook. All the boys carry their notebooks on their hip, all the girls clutch theirs to their (tender) chests.

Much as a loathe it, Emma's snobbery has dripped like a slow IV into my veins.

Boys I think I want to date are descendants of Wausau's elite, but they are only interested in 1) their female counterparts or 2) girls who go all the way. I'm neither. Boys like Jerry or Carl, who turn scarlet when I flirt with them in class, I pity and rather despise.

But you have to go to prom.

The boy who invites me reaches my ear. He has kinky black hair set off by a spray of red acne across his forehead. His eyebrows leaf dandruff. He's sarcastic, a whiz at math, and socially nowhere, like me. I don't know he's Jewish because to me Jewish means rich, like owning Heinemann's, the oldest mercantile business in town, or Winkelman's, the trendiest. He doesn't.

I can't care less whether he's Jewish or not, though I'm a confirmed Presbyterian. Oh, those endless Sunday School hours squirming on a low hard chair, my Mary Janes pinching as I stare at the framed reproduction of "Christ at the Door" on the basement wall. Can that languid, blue-eyed blond really be a Jewish prophet? And if he *is* Jewish, what am *I* doing here? It's one of my great puzzles. Except for memorizing Old Testament books to a catchy waltz tune and enjoying Biblical stories like Ruth midst the alien corn, Sunday School leaves me disgracefully unmoved. We never get to the New Testament.

Years later, the lawyer I haphazardly choose from the Wausau telephone directory for my first divorce turns out to be my former Sunday School teacher. In a flash I'm back in the Presbyterian Church basement. Mr. Tredwell's office with its brown linoleum and "Christ at the Door" on the wall are exactly the same and I swear the chair he offers me is child-sized. He squares his fingers in an imitation of our Presbyterian Church tower and frowns.

"If you'd attended Sunday School more often, Margo, this wouldn't have happened."

"If I'd heard the truth about anything," I burn to say, "I might have come."

All my life, above my head accompanying my every step, is a cloud fat with words I've wanted to say. I love the French expression "esprit d'escalier": the retort that comes to you after a tongue-tied encounter as you descend the stairs. I'm brilliant, descending the stairs.

A block south of the Presbyterian is the Episcopalian Church, a beguiling structure of weathered stone, plaster, and cross-beams. I *love* anything English. (*James!*) One priest I remember is Father John. Mother is smitten in a sweet, dopey way. He invites us to his "digs" to introduce her to martinis (I get a Coke). Having chilled two glasses in his freezer, he pours gin from a brown bottle of Bols into two martini glasses. Over twin lakes of gin he sprays a breath of vermouth from a small vial. He then strikes a match, touches it to a strip of lemon rind which yields four drops that he divides meticulously between the glasses. I feel I should kneel and pray. I know he's gay, though I don't know the word. Poor Elsie.

Now I rush down the stairs from the Presbyterian choir loft and dash the block to St. John's Christmas Eve service, which swankily begins at eleven. Slipping into a back row, I press my forehead to a wooden pew. The organ begins to prey upon my senses—not the robust "All Christian Men Rejoice" I've just sung at Presbyterian—no; but a melody in a mysterious minor key that makes me ache with tragic longings.

Tassels swinging from black velvet caps, the choir launches itself down the crimson-carpeted aisle. I almost miss Eunice Okoneski's wink as she slow-steps by because "O Come Emanuel" is tearing my heart out by the roots. I vow to be pure, a hero, not sass Elsie, not skip Sunday School, not kill Emma. Boys in white tunics and black skirts follow the choir, swinging brass coffers wafting clouds of incense that I inhale until I choke.

Oh, yes: Junior Prom.

On Emma's long hit list, Jews rank number two, just below Catholics. Every day that drags toward prom seems like 100 hours.

Neither of us has the guts to tell Emma I'm going, yet we fall over each other trying to give the game away. Mother spills my prom dress out of its box at Emma's feet. I intercept the florist at the front door, but Ben X.'s card falls into Emma's hands. Next morning she serves me my oatmeal in a bowl topped with scraps of his card. At the stove she's burning bacon. Her back is broad; a stench of rancid fat hangs in the air. Prom seems absurd.

Prom eve, the scent of American-Beauty Bubble Bath from our four-legged tub is overwhelming and I can hear Emma downstairs snuffling like a hound. Humming "When You Wish Upon a Star," Mother fastens twisty nylons to my new sateen garter belt. I squeeze my feet into the size six white shoes Emma bought me last summer because *"Young ladies don't wear sevens."*

Ben X. won't pick me up until seven. Downstairs at the dining room table, Elsie and I stare blankly at pork and cabbage, under my bathrobe my prom dress rustling like dry leaves. I'm to meet Ben, driven by his father, at Tenth and Washington.

"Tell your father our driveway's too steep to turn round in."

"No driveway fazes *my* dad."

"Just pick me up at the corner, okay?"

Upstairs in Emma's house there's no long mirror to show me what I look like. Elsie pats my shoulders with Tabu powder until I choke. I look down. My new breasts are crushed flat as pancakes.

"I can't wear this!"

"Actresses often wear costumes that don't fit. Pretend you look gorgeous. Act gorgeous. You *are* gorgeous."

I creep downstairs. In her chair in the front parlor, chin on chest, Emma seems oblivious to some comic's patter on the Philco. I glide across the room and test the doorknob. It doesn't turn. I tiptoe to the kitchen; the back door is locked. These locks open with a big key Emma keeps on a shelf above the kitchen stove. I run my hand along the tacky surface. No key.

Ben X. has become desirable.

Snatching my dress above my knees, I race upstairs. Mother is at her blue dressing table overlooking the garden. *"Blue skies, smiling at me . . . ."* Elevating her hand mirror, she's spanking her neck purposefully with the backs of her fingers. She turns to me, shrugs.

"I know, honey. Maybe it's for the best."

"*For the best?* Forty-five dollars we don't have for a dress that doesn't fit and it's for the best?"

I stalk to my room. My Baby Ben says ten past seven.

It's May and the storm windows are still on, fastened outside by wing nuts. I pace. The Underwood Aunt Marie gave me for my birthday sits on my desk. I haven't learned to type yet; it begs to be used. I hesitate, seize it, smash the lower pane of the storm and undo the wing nuts without severing a vein. I walk my hands up the frame; it's fastened at the top. Shoving half-heartedly at first, then with purpose, I feel the storm giving. It tilts and falls away into space.

Emma's house sits on a narrow lot cut into the cheek of East Hill. Under my window rises the neighbor's lawn, a drop of maybe seven feet, I'm bad at measuring distances. I stow the gardenia corsage I've kept on the window sill to keep fresh in my pocket, crawl onto the sill and launch myself into twilight. The landing shocks me from soles to scalp.

I hobble down the hill, toes thrusting against my shoe tips. It's evening now. A street lamp strung on wires above Tenth and Washington flings shadows up and down the empty crossroad. I hover unsure at the curb, then decide to pace up and down so I look as though I'm going somewhere. I linger half an hour, praying for the arrival of Ben X and his Dad who isn't fazed by anything. When I pull the gardenia out of my pocket, its petals are brown.

Somewhere over on Jefferson a barn owl cries. I trudge back up the hill, try Emma's door. Locked. I huddle on the porch steps, yanking my short pink coat around my knees. Can a healthy thirteen-year-old freeze to death on a mid-May night in north-central Wisconsin? Neighborhood houses show lights, but I wouldn't dream of knocking at a door.

What could I say?

Tomorrow the uphill neighbor will find smashed glass. He'll collect the shards so his five children won't cut themselves, then knock at Emma's door.

"Found this glass on our lawn this morning, Mrs. Merkel. Ain't mine, must be yours. " He's afraid of her.

"I know nothing about glass on your lawn."

Scratching his head. "I can fix the winda if you like."

"My son John will take care of it."

Did Ben go to the prom without me? I see the gym I spent hours helping decorate with balloons and red and white streamers, couples shuffling cheek to cheek to "Now Is the Hour," guys guzzling Cokes and punching each other, in the john girls leaning into the mirror twirling pageboys around their fingers.

The owl hoots again, nearer this time—"*Kee-yow! Wow! Kee-yow! Wow!*" I uncramp my legs and walk down to the drive, hoping to see something familiar like the Big Dipper. There it is, sparking above the apple trees—and Orion too.

A car chugs up the hill, passes the house but doesn't turn around. Not Ben X. coming to rescue me. My toes are dead. I pee in the bushes, I wet my new silk stockings.

Hours later the porch light shatters the night like a bright knife. I hear a key grind in the lock. When I creep into the house, Emma is invisible.

CHAPTER EIGHTEEN

I'm lying across my bed, Elsie's brushing my hair.

"I've got to see the movie at the Grand this afternoon."

"Honey, no, you see too many movies."

"But it's Bette Davis."

"It'll play for a week."

"I want to see it today."

"Now, Honey—"

I grab the hairbrush from her hand, hurl it at her, bang out of the room. I jump on my bike, zoom down the hill, buy two boxes of Junior Mints and prepare for a Bette Davis orgy.

All I can think of is the punishment waiting at home.

Actually I want it. I want her to jump up, square off with me face to face. I want her to grab my shoulders, shake me and say: "Look here, just because I asked you to call me Elsie doesn't mean I'm not your mother and goddamn well the boss here."

These words she can't speak.

I find her at her dressing table, overwhelmed as usual by boxes of scraps, notes, bills, theater programs, letters. Dozens of letters. She's wondering what to do with them.

"Hey, Elsie," my new motherless self says. "I can solve this."

Grabbing two boxes of letters, I run downstairs. Into the primed fireplace I drop a match, into the blaze I toss sheet after sheet. Does Elsie fly downstairs, snatch the boxes from my hand, slap me silly, ground me for a month?

From time to time she taps at the window with a fingernail, her frowning round face pressed against the pane. Light and shadow wash the glass, as if she's speaking underwater. I don't want to hear and don't stop until every letter is ash.

Looking back, I know that on that day of flinging a hairbrush and of cruel, furious burning I emotionally stopped being Elsie McCullough's daughter.

Two events, plus the traumas of years, create what happens this summer.

It's May, a few weeks before school lets out, Elsie's left for work, I'm standing in the kitchen in blouse and slip, waiting for Emma to finish ironing a blue cotton skirt I'll wear to school today. Emma rams the smoking iron back and forth across the helpless fabric.

"Aunt Hattie, you know?" She gives me glare.

"Yes?"

"Tell me the truth. Have you ever heard her say *one good thing* about anybody?"

I stare at my shoes and wait for my skirt.

"Tears people to pieces what's she does. Mean, snake-shit mean. *Hypocrite*. Never a kind word for her kin, never a kind word for anybody."

I take a breath and say, far too wisely: "People always blame others for what they hate most in themselves."

A sudden tigress behind the ironing board hurls the iron at me. Its hot point gouges my right calf. I yelp and stare down to see a small, deep-carved triangle with a lot of yellow stuff I recognize as fat tissue beginning to well with blood.

I run upstairs, ball up toilet paper, press it against the wound. Then I remember big bandages in the closet left over from the time Johnny cut his hand sickling the overgrown back yard. I find one, wind it around my leg, tie a knee sock around it to hold it in place. I yank on a pair of jeans, hop on my bicycle and make it to school as the last bell rings.

My home room teacher is Roland Johnson. Elsie is his friend, along with Eunice Okoneski, who teaches art at Central School, Vida Okoneski, and Noël Seim. I remember the Sunday they took me along to tea in Mr. Johnson's Japanese-style apartment and I had to use his bathroom. Red tile, black bathtub, black toilet, black sink, red towels. Tiny, tortured trees growing out of blood-red ceramic bowls.

Six-feet-five, Mr. Johnson towers over us students. He wears elegant suits—grey in winter, fawn in spring. His daffodil and raspberry shirts are perfectly finished by silver, sky-blue or orange-sherbet ties. Out of respect for his friendship with Elsie (and his occasional wink) I do not, like the others, call him "Madame Butterfly." Today I rely on my social connections. Behind his desk, I roll up a jean leg, display my mess. Paling, he shoos me away with a carefully manicured hand to the school nurse.

I heal, most things heal. But I told Elsie, who wrote Marie. This was the same May I did not go to the prom with Ben X. Ben happened to be equipped with a Jewish mother who, after the prom, called Elsie at the Record Herald and gave her such extended hell that Elsie was jolted into telephoning Marie in Milwaukee. Now she waves a letter under my nose.

"Put down your book, Margo, this is from Marie. I've told her everything. Listen: 'Margo has got to get out of the house. She *cannot* live with Grandmother any longer.'"

I try to take this in. "Swell. But where do I go?"

"Marie has a plan."

A few weeks later I sit in a Wausau High classroom bent over a terrifying aptitude exam that will qualify me for a scholarship to the prestigious private high school Milwaukee Downer Seminary. A scholarship is the only way I can attend such an expensive private girls' school.

Dilemma. I'm too proud to deliberately blow the test, *but Milwaukee Downer Seminary?* Hard to say which is more terrifying, Downer or Emma. Marie says a *C* at Downer is an *A* at Wausau High. Above all, girls from Milwaukee's wealthiest families attend Downer. This is going to be Mrs. Murray's Dancing Class twenty-four-seven for three years. Not to mention I'll have to exchange my Wausau friends for strict hours, chaperones, home only for holidays. I pray I flunk the tests, I pray I don't.

In early July I open a manila envelope and extract a catalogue stamped with a white crest:

MILWAUKEE DOWNER SEMINARY. SIT LUX.

I'm so intimidated I look up *sit lux* in the dictionary Aunt Marie just gave me as a junior high graduation present. "Let there be light."

I open the catalogue. "For almost 100 years Milwaukee Downer has been conscious of its responsibility in the cultural, spiritual, and social aspects of secondary life. The 57 graduates of the class of 1948 all gained admission to colleges of their choice. Records such as this give assurance that our girls may depend upon competent teaching to prepare them adequately for broader fields of endeavor, and upon intelligent counseling and guidance to help them find themselves."

The letter is from Nar Warren Taylor, Headmistress: "I am delighted to be welcoming you to Milwaukee Downer Seminary this fall."

This is going to be far more fun than Mrs. Murray's Dancing Class.

In preparation for Downer Elsie and I go shopping, which involves strategies only slightly less complex than General Eisenhower marshaled for D-Day. I need good outfits because the Seminary abolished uniforms the year before. Elsie can't afford good outfits. Under sullen, sweltering August skies we toil Wausau's downtown.

"Not Livingston's, I haven't paid them a dime since February."

"But that darling knit suit in the window!"

"Never mind. Let's try Miljay's Bridal. I haven't charged there since May."

The look on the face of the saleslady, dressed beyond her wages in pearls and navy crepe, contradicts Elsie's claim. Placing one tiny pump behind the other, she retreats from Elsie's false bright smile.

"My daughter's been accepted at the most exclusive girls' school in the Midwest. She needs a few things to go away with ... ."

I squirm as Elsie makes lordly purchases. We leave with two nightgowns, one robe, three slips, three bras, and six pairs of lace-trimmed panties. On account.

But I need blouses, skirts, dresses. Heineman's Department Store is our last hope. Perhaps because the Heinemans have been key players in Wausau's early economy, they're less uptight about credit than Sam Winkelman, the silver-haired gentleman with a white mustache who mercilessly sweats his female employees. (I made forty-five cents an hour the three summers I clerked at Winkelman's. Great-Aunt Elsie, in charge of dry goods for three decades, earned sixty-five.)

Ben Heineman Jr is never anything but gracious. "Please show Mrs. McCullough and her daughter the new line of fall school clothes." We seem to be treated with the respect Heinemann's would pay Alexanders, Yawkeys and Woodsons. Perhaps Ben Heineman knows Elsie will spend more than all three millionaires put together.

We emerge with plaid and navy skirts, cashmere sweaters, an *adorable* leaf-brown corduroy suit studded with leather buttons, a navy-blue wool dress for Sundays. But a big purchase still has to be made. Elsie looks worried; then brightens.

"I know, I can open an account at Schmidt's! They've got darling things!"

"We can't!"

"You have to have a coat."

I trail her miserably up the steps into the upscale ladies-wear store on Sixth Street.

"Choose, something, darling, while I fill out these forms," she says gaily. "We can afford it!"

I pretend interest in the racks of clothes we can't buy, I clank hangers nervously. And then I see it: a camel hair coat with a taffy silk lining, smart pockets, beautifully cut lapels. Sixty-five dollars: two weeks of Elsie's salary, plus. I don't care.

"Yes, well, it's a *classic*, isn't it," says the patronizing clerk.

"I can see that," says Elsie, goaded. "Box it up, please."

Emma looks over her newspaper as we stagger in.

"High-falutin' scheis-hoppers! Spending without a cent to your name. Could have made everything myself!"

How *does* Emma feel about my going away? Theoretically she should rejoice that my foot is now planted on a rung of the social ladder she still worships. Yet we've been together fifteen years. Is it possible she'll miss me? Besides, she's deeply conservative, hates change, "rail-riding," she calls it. "East, west—home's best," she croons, with no sense of irony. Maybe she'll miss yelling at me mornings, throwing hot irons. Oh, well, she still has Elsie to kick around. On the day I'm set to leave her house, I'm chiefly thinking of my own skin.

That September seventh Elsie and I are taking the train to Milwaukee; my bags and boxes are packed; my new dark-green travel dress laid out alongside new low pumps, hat, and white gloves. The house is still, though I know early-riser Emma prowls below. "And when she saw you in your new sailor-suit," I hear Elsie saying, "she fell to the floor with a heart attack. I couldn't leave. We never met Edgar in Chicago."

Will she fall to the floor with a heart attack today? If she does, will I go or stay? Known terrors are preferable to unknown. Almost I hope she'll gasp and crumple so I'll have to call the ambulance and take care of her forever.

At breakfast, not a word. I retreat to my room, distractedly tidy drawers and stow loved objects I can't take with me in my big trunk along with Sonja Heine, my expensive Madame Alexander doll, Betsy-Wetsy, Raggedy Ann, Story Book dolls, Judy Bolton mysteries, and my now bulging James Mason scrapbook. Foolish toys, childish toys—farewell. My sick stomach feels sicker.

At noon I open my door and hear Elsie downstairs at the telephone trying to order a cab. She's whispering, how they possibly hear her?

I haul my huge suitcase downstairs. Front or side door? Front is a longer haul, but I can't get down the side without entering Emma's kitchen. I've no idea where she is. I open the kitchen door. Emma's sitting on her stool listening to Frankie Yankovich or the Three Fat Dutchmen, I never can tell the difference. She doesn't look at me. A horn squawks in the drive.

"Bye, Mother." Elsie over my shoulder, bright and desperate as always. "Margo wants to say goodbye." She nudges me forward, but I'm rooted.

"Goodbye, Grandmother."

Deliberately, Emma turns her back on me. I see how much of her thick, curly, upswept hair is still soot-black. I see her Lane Bryant Catalogue print cotton housedress obscenely caught between her big buttocks. I hate her.

"I'll write," I croak and dash from the house.

The cab's pulling away when I think I see a motion at the kitchen window. Trick of light, reflection of moving branches? Emma?

I wave.

CHAPTER NINETEEN

Elsie and I arrive in a cab. Cadillacs and mile-long Town and Country station wagons line the curb, decanting Milwaukee Downer boarders and their baggage.

A grey sky does nothing to warm brick buildings the color of dried blood. I take in Gothic arches, mullioned bay windows, forests of ivy creeping up venerable walls. This is how I imagine olde England to be. Alas, James is not escorting me, black steed nickering to my white mare, to his castle.

Flanking a Gothic door, two women wait to welcome us. Mrs. Holmes is a tiny, svelte lady in gray tweed, with a worried face and twisted lip, one hand wrapped around a bottle of Coca-Cola. Mrs. Welch is a motherly dumpling with untidy gray hair in a bun and knitting needles poking out the pocket of her cardigan.

Our entrance is a panic attack in slow motion. Girls surge past us—hugging, kissing, yelling—while parents, younger sibs and porters with luggage shoulder us aside. Strange perfumes hit me—chrysanthemums, old wood, new wax. My bag is grabbed by a powerful woman with a broad, unsmiling face—a maid, I guess, since she's wearing a white uniform. (I've never seen a maid before.) She toils ahead up a wide staircase, turns right. At the end of a long corridor she throws open a door. I step into my dorm room, an 8 x 12 rectangle painted utility-white. Bed, desk, bureau, cork bulletin board and small closet, that's it. Elsie pats her hair in the mirror over the bureau. "Honey, you're going to love it here." We hug and she leaves, in debt for the rest of her life.

She's staying with Marie a couple of days before returning to Wausau. The land that Wau saw. I long to see it now.

A knock and a blond page-boy thrusts into my room.

"I'm Helen, your Old Girl."

Helen! How I wish she were *my* Helen.

"Every New Girl gets an Old Girl to show her the ropes. Dinner's casual tonight, no nylons, no seating assignment, come as you are. Nights like this Cook always serves Sloppy Joes. Everything okee-dokee so far?"

"So far."

"Swell. See you in Hall."

These are the first and last words I exchange with my Old Girl.

I make up my bed with the new denim spread Marie bought me from Gimbel's, climb onto the bed to hang matching candy-striped curtains at the single window. I want to enshrine the glossy 8 X 10 James Mason photo I've autographed "To Margo with my passionate love" on the bulletin board, but am terrified I'll be laughed at. Instead I tack up a snapshot of the popular Hoffman twins, a photo of me sitting in Johnny's robin's-egg blue convertible, and—for morale—a tiny Kodak of Patrick Kennedy and me cuddling on Emma's steps.

My window looks on the front lawn and that dried-blood building that must be the school itself. Only a block away I can see cars moving along Downer Avenue, *free*. From Lake Michigan a foghorn moans. Black crows flap into the oak outside my window, settle like bad omens.

I discover that the whole school knows that two boarders are scholarship students: a pleasant, pretty girl named Barbara; and me. Barbara gets the message. Scholarship students earn their keep with superior grades, good behavior, toothy smiles, and devoted service. Unfortunately, I haven't the least concept of *owing* Milwaukee Downer anything. On the contrary, I blame Emma—and obscurely Downer—for my being here at all.

Those first weeks I map the Dorm's geography: big dark infirmary just down the hall from me, institution-size bathroom next to the stairs, Mrs. Welch's room, where she sits knitting and smiling, just past the staircase. We eat in "Hall," an enormous room lit by high windows, with walls hung with "antique" escutcheons. I find it my first evening by trailing other boarders downstairs to discover my Old Girl Helen cosy with friends at a far table. Panicking, I slip into the first empty chair. To the chrysanthemum and waxed-floor perfume is now added the pervasive smell of food: food to be cooked, cooking, past cooked. What a pity it doesn't kill my appetite. I'd like to shed ten pounds.

Vera, a no-nonsense, middle-aged woman in a white uniform, is like Control Tower to O'Hare. In her tiny office tucked left of Hall stairs, her face registers neither alarm nor sympathy. We stop at Vera's for everything. Vera, where's my missing laundry? Vera, has my boy friend called? Vera, what's this pink slip from Mrs. Holmes! Just *one minute* late for check-in, fix it, Vera, *please*?

Past Vera's headquarters stand a clutch of much-used telephone booths and a table with a lamp like a spotlight. This table bears the sign-out book. I discover that this book is like Webster's Dictionary or the Bible, only far more important.

I submit to the daily routine:

6:15 rise
7:15 breakfast
8:00 chapel
8:15-11:15 classes
11:15 study hall
12:15 lunch
1:15-4:15 classes
4:15 FREE
5:15 study
6:15 dinner
7:00 FREE
7:30 study
10:30 lights out

Weird to say, I'm elected dorm vice-president. I make friends with freshmen and juniors, ominously not with anyone in my sophomore class except a large sarcastic girl named Mary Connor. After classes (unless kept after for algebra) I breeze down Downer Avenue with Sandy Jones and Robin Wrezin to the drugstore to devour hot fudge sundaes topped with whipped cream and pecans hot from a roaster. I join the Riding Club. The Riding Club gets to eat at a separate table Friday evenings because we reek. (Who's paying for my jodhpurs and boots, not to mention riding fees?) I go to all the dances, all the skating parties, hear Vladimir Horowitz play Chopin at the Pabst, scream with laughter at Beatrice Lillie (*"Chickasaw boom, Chickasaw boom, women wear falsies in their bazoom"*), thrill to Judith Anderson as lethal Medea, adore suave Maurice Evans in *Man and Superman.*

Like all boarders, I go down to dinner in laddered nylons concealed under a black ballerina skirt. Unlike other boarders I'm publicly reproved for pushing food onto my fork with my knife and conveying it to my mouth with my left hand. "I eat the British way," I explain. Like all the boarders I eventually get sung to at dinner:

How do you do, Margo McCullough,
How do you do?
Is there anything that we can do for you?
We'll take you by the hand,
Stand by you like a man.
How do you do, Margo McCullough,
How do you do!

I learn the jargon. If Wausau was "cool," "neat," and "smooth," Downer's "a panic," "swingin'," or "hangin' right in there." A sarcastic reply is "a bitter thrust." Dorm rooms are "miserable hovels." We shoot down stupid remarks with "No shit, Dick Tracy," abbreviated to "N.S.D.T."

Like all boarders, I pin photos of liquor bottles, sports cars, puppies, movie stars, and St. John's Military Academy boys on my bulletin board, along with dead corsages, ticket stubs, and souvenir football programs. Like most (just guessing) I boast of non-existent boyfriends back home. I jive in the halls to "The Johnson Rag" and thrill to Charles Trenet's "La Mer" throbbing from portable phonographs all down the hall. After lights I sneak into rooms to gobble brownies from home and natter about boys.

Coca-Cola Holmes and Grandma Welch know all, of course.

Some Day Girls are grinds, there because of Downer's academic reputation. Some come from wealthy Milwaukee families like the Uihleins, Pabsts, and Bradleys. I already know them from Mrs. Murray's Dancing Class: blond page-boys, trim waists, intimidating self-confidence. Slouching through the conservatory mornings, I see them pulling up in their Packard and Buick convertibles; first day of classes, they foam arm-in-arm up the old staircases. I hadn't counted on the Day Girls.

But at this point classes are my big worry. "Compared to Downer Sem, Wausau High is *kindergarten*!" I write Elsie on Downer stationery. I'm sweating over Latin, algebra, biology, history, English, and French. I have some aptitude for English and French; but French, taught by Mademoiselle Wittmer, *une vrai française* with snapping black eyes and a sooty mustache, is formidable; and English, with two essays a week, not exactly a snap.

"You write like Virginia Woolf," says Miss Mary Zeller, handing back my first theme.

Suspecting a compliment, I fly to the library to identify V. Woolf. Pulling a book called *To the Lighthouse* from the shelf, I open it at random:

> Hours he would spend thus, with his pipe, of an evening, thinking up and down and in and out of the old familiar lanes and commons, which were all stuck about with the history of that campaign there, the life of this statesman here, with poems and with anecdotes, with figures too, this thinker, that soldier; all very brisk and clear; but at length the lane, the field, the common, the fruitful nut-tree and the flowering hedge led him on to that further turn of the road where he dismounted always, tied his horse to a tree, and proceeded on foot alone.

I stand there transfixed. I don't write like Virginia Woolf, I don't *understand* like Virginia Woolf! How, for instance, can she presume to know what an elderly man is thinking? (Emma: "Men have only one thing on their minds.") But oh if only I *could* write like this. For a shining moment the possibility of an author's life opens before me, illuminated by flood-lights and soaring music. I envision my pen racing, paragraphs of immortal prose taking shape under my hand. I check out *To the Lighthouse* and that night after study hall launch upon my voyage of discovery. Fifteen minutes later I'm asleep. I haven't a clue what Virginia Woolf is talking about.

Teachers have always been VIPs in my world, maybe because at 1016 only Emma was *in loco parentis* and I fought her. I try to obey teachers, work hard for their approval, speculate about their private lives, get terrific crushes on a few.

Downer Sem teachers seem a different breed. Some, like the mathematician Miss Matheny, crawl into class like ancient tortoises, wattles of skin swinging from their chins, eyes weeping, legs bandaged—years past public school retirement age.

Most are middle-aged unmarried women, though my algebra teacher Charlotte Main is a type I never knew in Wausau, nor do I know the term "dyke". Tall and square-shouldered, with level brows and jutting chin, she strides into class slapping a ruler against a hard palm. Personalized Massachusetts license plates on her Dodge testify she hasn't had an accident in twenty-five years. She never takes chaperone duty. She is the toughest teacher at Downer and obviously the brainiest. Too bad I'm too terror-stricken to fully admire her qualities.

Then there are the widows and divorcees, or rather for Mary Connor and me, one divorcee, Madame Van Wagenen—Madame because she also teaches French. Her real name is Margaret and she lives off-campus, which makes her seem infinitely glamorous compared to teachers serving time in the dorm.

Madame has knowing pale blue eyes hooded by lids thick as mushroom caps. She wears soft suits with nipped-in waists and stiletto heels with ankle straps. Girls whisper that Madame's high heels have so deformed her calves that barefoot she has to walk on tiptoe. She sweeps up her light brown hair and pins it in two fluffy rolls on top of her head that dip to a *V* over her forehead, making her face a valentine. She is haughty, humorous, worldly: the only woman remotely approaching my exacting Davis-Crawford-Stanwyck standard.

I'll have Madame for second semester English.

At first Chapel I get a look at the woman behind the signature on the Downer stationery. Nar Warren Taylor, Head Mistress, towers over the assembly. Short auburn hair clings to her scalp in disciplined waves. She has white skin, green eyes, a classic nose. Dimples dent her white cheeks like whirlpools; her chin is large and firm. She wears a pale green suit with pearls. Below a mid-calf skirt her ankles are aristocratic.

When she opens her mouth I'm surprised to hear a molasses-thick Southern drawl. My skin prickles, I don't know why. She is the executive woman, a type I admire. Or is she Emma—Emma empowered by education, a prestigious school, and a good salary instead of wild, personal force? Perhaps it's the way Miss Taylor's tight mouth denies her lazy vowels? Watch out, I think: she will be the iron fist in the velvet glove; and then we all stand to sing "Jerusalem."

CHAPTER TWENTY

Elsie's waiting when the Hiawatha pulls into the Wausau Depot. I note critically that she's still wearing the pillbox and squirrel-trim coat, forgetting that she's so deep in hock for my Downer clothes she'll be wearing them to her grave. Marie paid for my trip home. Hungry, I'd stared hard at passengers on their way to the club car, hoping one would invite an interesting young lady to lunch. No one did, so I amused myself by adopting an upper-class British accent (courtesy James Mason) and enthralling a middle-aged couple opposite with tales of barely surviving the London Blitz.

I hop off the train, unfortunately tailed by my audience. I embrace Elsie and lock eyes. "I've been boring these lovely people with London, Mummy," I say brightly, "—*you know*, during the Blitz." "Ah, the Blitz." Elsie's British accent is flawless. "Margo here insisted on staying with her wounded father during the darkest days of the war." "So brave," murmur the couple, thankfully moving off to retrieve their luggage.

"Let's walk," says Elsie cheerfully. I guess she can't afford a cab, now thirty-five cents, and I long ago spent my weekly three-dollar allowance. Between us we lug my suitcase up Scott Street, Elsie, though she's only thirty-six, panting like a raced horse. At Stewart's Park she has to stop.

Stewart's is still magic, though not as vastly mysterious as I remembered. Elsie plunks herself down on a stone wall and toes-off a brown-suede shoe streaked white with scuff-marks.

"Look." I extend the right sleeve of the fabulous, still unpaid for polo coat. Black holes scallop the right cuff.

She doesn't get it. She'd also been oblivious to the long nicotine-high of my eleventh summer, spent in Mary Jane Hovden's chicken shed smoking cigarettes in garish flat packs of five that her Navy brother brought back from Japan. In May his duffel bag was tight as a sausage; late August it sagged. We *can't* have smoked that many cigarettes.

"After class during Free Time we sneak down alleys for a cigarette. Sometimes we have to cuff 'em because teachers patrol." I demonstrate the Downer technique of flipping a cigarette up my sleeve. I try to sound nonchalant, but I feel awful about the beautiful polo coat.

Yet I can admit to smoking because she's no longer my mother, she's Elsie. By now I feel like her elder sister, a passage that may have happened the day she brought home a Monet reproduction from Kresge's Dime Store: two women in a boat, the younger oaring, the elder leaning back to be rowed. "That's us," said Elsie. "You're rowing our boat."

"What do you mean! I can't row my own boat, let alone yours."

She laughs now, takes out a pack of Pall Malls from her purse, thumbs the package until two white cylinders rise above their mates. I produce Milwaukee Zebra Lounge matches, sing a Downer ditty as I light us up:

> Matches, matches,
> M-A-T-C-H-E-S.
> Matches, matches,
> M-A-T-C-H-E-S.
> Strike 'em in the toilets
> Strike 'em in the halls
> I know a boy who can
> Strike 'em on his—

O god, it's so *good* to be out of that hovel. I spit a thread of tobacco, inhale deeply. Our smoke mingles in the November air with the sweet resin of white pines.

Then I remember. Emma.

My Blitz story must have been a rehearsal for horrors to come. Have I missed my grandmother since I've been gone? Oddly, yes. Not the daily terror but little things. Her chuckle, her rhymes, her singing "I Dreamt I Dwelt in Marble Halls" while I play the piano. But suddenly I realize we're dawdling not only because Elsie wants a smoke but because Emma's on the warpath; and do I know this warpath. Yet seen from the distance of Milwaukee Downer, ruled by seemingly rational beings, Emma seems grotesque. Why are Elsie and I lugging my suitcase up the hill to this disaster, this Armageddon—as family holidays are sure to be?

"Couldn't we have spent Thanksgiving at Marie's?" I know the answer. We don't dare.

Emma is wearing Grandfather's baggy tan cardigan with the broken button and permanent grease stains. Bending to brush her hair with my lips, I smell lilac cologne. Somehow I'm touched. She's dressed up for me.

"Too swelligans to kiss your old Grandma?"

She'll smell cigarettes, but I kiss her powdery-silk cheek. At sixty-five her skin is unwrinkled: opaque, poreless, sagging only slightly under her chin, which gives her a kind of FDR authority.

Her nostrils flare, but she only smiles secretly. Coming Soon: Main Feature: Hellza Poppin.

Elsie has scuttled to a radiator and I'm reminded that the house is always cold. I haul my suitcase upstairs and look around my alien room. It's not much larger than my cell at Downer Sem.

Next day Johnny arrives in a Lincoln Continental borrowed from a Washington friend we know only as "Austin the Rich."

He kisses Emma's cheek.

"Gosh, you're looking great, Mother."

"Compared to what?"

"To my girlfriends, darling. You know you're beautifulest of 'em all."

"Never get a straight word out of a rail-rider, never will."

Johnny shoves a fat gold-wrapped box of Whitman's Sampler into her hands. They share a terrific sweet tooth.

"My Lincoln's your chariot, Best Girl. Say the word, we're off."

"The graves need flowers."

"Isn't it *lovely*?" Thin Marie, cabbing up unmet from the Depot on a later train, wrings her hands. "Together for Thanksgiving—the whole Fandamily!"

I get it. Damn family.

Grandfather's home for the holiday and playing cards at the Eagles. He's not won a schauskopf hand in living memory, but a man's club is his castle, where wives' phone calls ring unanswered in smoky, indifferent rooms.

Trouble begins that evening when Mr. Schumacher, owner of the Fair Deal Grocery, delivers a turkey that weighs twenty pounds.

Emma dimples, trying to cover her huge stomach with a kitchen towel. Mr. Schumacher, though apparently a religious nut, is a looker.

"You have it wrong, Mr. Schumacher. I ordered a fifteen-pound bird."

Grandfather shuffles and bites the stem of his cold pipe.

"Pound or two, Mrs. Merkel—what the difference? You got a family to feed."

"Sure," says Grandfather. "Pound or two, after all it's Thanksgiving."

"It's not a pound or two, Mr. Schumacher, it's five pounds at eighteen cents a pound, which makes ninety cents more I have to pay you." She glares at her husband. He's always to blame for the turkey. "Do *you* have ninety cents, Cheapskate?"

He inflates empty pockets, does a hopeless Chaplin two-step.

Marie rushes in, pays the difference, wishes Mr. Schumacher the best of Thanksgivings, Christmases, New Years, Decades, Centuries.

When the whole family's home, Elsie sleeps with me, Marie takes Elsie's blue room, and Johnny makes do with the living room couch. Presumably Emma sleeps with her husband; I don't care to know. Scrunching away from Elsie to the edge of the mattress, I try not to think of tomorrow, but of touring green England with James Mason in our open Rolls Royce Silver Ghost. But James has lost his spell.

I'm routed out of bed by Emma at eight a.m. "What did I tell that Schumacher? The turkey's too big!"

"Let me try." I manage to force the bird into the roaster. Emma and I hoist it between us, but the turkey sticks halfway into the oven.

"Eastern shyster can't buy me an oven that holds a twenty-pound turkey."

Emma calls us "shyster" less often than "rail-rider" or "Indian." We're used to it, along with her accusation that all Merkels are Jews.

I grit my teeth and shove the turkey into the oven, savaging pale breastbone skin.

Elsie, Johnny and I play Authors on the round cherrywood table in the living room. Too nervous to play games, Marie flits about in an apron tidying—in this house like treating a coronary with cod liver oil. Johnny's brought a bottle of Mogen David, his father's favorite. Unscrewing the top he splashes purple into the "good" family snifters.

"Lift your glasses, darlings, to health, wealth, and happiness."

"Next semester I get Mrs. Van Wagenen for English."

I don't say it, really, I'm just thinking. Marie's babbling like a liar on sodium pentothal, Johnny loudly rides her over, Elsie vaguely but insistently chimes in. In this family I don't have a chance to utter, seldom have had the chance.

Grandfather ambles in, hands behind his back.

"Guess it's time to test the turkey."

To Emma her husband's testing the turkey is firing the first shot in the Revolutionary War.

"Have a glass, Grandfather! I'm pouring your favorite wine."

"Can't take wine this early in the day, doesn't sit well on my stomach."

"Come play cards with us."

"Don't know the game you're playing."

"We'll teach you. Or I know, let's play checkers!"

"Emma roasts the juice out of the bird if I don't stop her." With either great bravery or misplaced trust, he leaves for the kitchen.

"Do you have *The House of Seven Gables?*" I ask brightly. But Johnny's ear is toward the kitchen.

In this house everything can be heard. "Eastern shit-monger! Home two days a year and tells me how to cook the Thanksgiving turkey, never lifts a finger in this house and we're starving? *Elsie* slaves eight to five to pay for our food. *And he presumes to tell me when the turkey's done?*"

A crash, a hellish chorus of spitting fat.

"I'll go." Marie's teeth are chattering.

"Sit down, Sis, says Johnny. "I'll handle this."

I fling down my cards, take two stairs at a time, slam my bedroom door, jam my fingers into my ears. As I've done *ad infinitum.* Youth in this house has been *ad infinitum.*

Later, through my radiator, comes the sound of Emma assaulting the furnace with a poker as she tosses coals into the pit.

We never eat Thanksgiving dinner.

Johnny spends hours on his knees scrubbing the grease-slicked kitchen floor with ammonia and All-Brite. Grandfather's right hand is bandaged. Next day Marie and I escape on the Hiawatha. I sleep on her couch two nights and cab to Milwaukee Downer Sunday morning, the first boarder in the empty dorm. I'm sick with guilt for leaving Johnny because he doesn't come home that often. For Elsie and Grandfather I feel both sorrow and scorn. They have chosen their fates.

On Monday a letter from Elsie:

Shocking and horrid! Johnny left Sunday in the Lincoln, though how humiliated and repentant I can only guess. Not his fault, of course, but on Friday in his zeal to *bring our home up to his high standards,* he waxed the cellar stairs. As he does his car, naturally, though I've never heard of waxing cellar stairs? Then off he went to see old pals and I walked to work Saturday morning (half day, hurrah!).

Grandmother, unaware of Johnny's efforts, started down to tend the furnace. According to her outraged report, her legs flew out from under her and down she went head over heels. The poor thing lay on the cold cellar floor until well past five when I got home, having stopped to visit Alice. I called Dr. Smith immediately.

"You're a tough old bird, Mrs. Merkel," he said. Not polite (especially after Th. turkey), but *true*.

You'll be delighted to hear that your Grandmother is resting comfortably. She asks about you every minute: "How is Margo, etc. etc." She is strangely anxious about your return for Christmas, as (Marie?) has intimated you might spend Christmas holidays elsewhere? This may cause great distress, etc.

Lovingly, Elsie.

P.S. Grandfather was at the Eagles and got home after I did.

Johnny waxed the cellar stairs, knowing that only his mother uses them regularly. Johnny the rose-sending son. I'd feel some remorse, except for my clear picture of Elsie bending to lipstick her mouth, the shattered front mirror, the spinning applesauce jar. Pity, in a way, that Johnny's plan didn't work. Oh, yes, I think deep in his core he wanted to do her harm.

CHAPTER TWENTY-ONE

From infancy I've experienced *male* as: a) charming, b) irresponsible, c) abject, d) divine, e) absent.

It stands to reason that at fifteen I'll be in deep trouble with boys. And I am.

Certainly I'm not obvious "date bait," as they call it. I'm five-feet-six with a thirty-six C bust, twenty-five-inch waist, and thirty-seven-inch hips. Boys look at figures first, which is the only reason I give my statistics; and from what I know, boys like cute, small, manageable girls they can flip around on dance floors and elsewhere. Faces matter to them less, not that mine's anything to brag about, though I've been called "the poor man's Elizabeth Taylor." (More like the pauper's, I'd say.) And I have a scar on my right cheek, "my dueling scar," as I defiantly call it. Gene Kelly has an identical scar, but he's a man. "I'm scarred," I tell myself dramatically, not meaning my small white cicatrix.

I have tons of energy and a pretty good sense of humor. There's no way I'd tell any boy how much I love books and classical music. (Any girl, either.) I may have some brains but I seldom use them. I'm not conventionally "feminine." This Aunt Marie informs me after administrating a test to determine Life Interests. The results distress her enough that she asks me to go for a walk.

"Well, Margo, you scored fifty-fifty."

My IQ can't be that low!

"Fifty per cent of your choices were female, fifty per cent male. Frankly, I'm worried." She throws me a glance. "Certainly your body is *all* female. But your answers!"

"That test!" I'm dismayed. "What would *you* say, Marie, asked whether you'd like to change dirty diapers or fly an airplane? Be a den mother or a professional pianist? Bake cookies or raft a river?"

And anyway what is her investment in this test? I can only conclude that her goal for me is to be a married housewife changing dirty diapers, den-mothering, and baking cookies. This from an unmarried aunt with a career!

A boy or two seems to find me attractive.

The August of 1948, before I enter Downer in September as a sophomore, Elsie and I are visiting Marie in Milwaukee in her (loaned) Art-Deco apartment on Prospect Avenue. One day we hike over to Bradford Beach on Lake Michigan. Elsie drops onto a towel and lights a cigarette. I pick my way into the iced turquoise water, ribs of hard white sand massaging the soles of my feet. Before I get waist deep I'm grabbed from behind, next thing I know I'm under.

"What the heck are you doing?" I scream when I surface.

A tall, stocky sunburned boy with a Marine crewcut and sapphire eyes shaded by black lashes long as broomsticks grins at me. "Aw," he says, "just kidding." He flings up his arms and back-flips. I watch his white legs describe an imperfect arc, hear his head hit hard bottom. He resurfaces coughing lake.

I stalk out of Lake Michigan, I *may* have wiggled my bum. Ten minutes later the same charmer approaches our beach towels, loaded with Cokes, hot dogs oozing mustard, and cartons of french fries. He squares his burned shoulders.

"Pleath accept my humble apologieth."

Elsie grinds out her cigarette in the sand.

"Have we met?"

A slight, darkly tanned boy with myopic chocolate-brown eyes ducks under the tall boy's arm.

"Ladies, you really must accept Donald Allan's apologies. He can't help it. He's a terrible nuisance but he's also completely generous and sincere. I can vouch for him."

Donald grins shyly. Elsie smiles. We invite sunburned and tanned to sit down, we devour fries, sip Cokes. Soon we're chattering like old friends.

Donald Allan's older sister Patsy is a Downer Seminary grad. His friend, Rob, is desolate because his lawyer father is moving the family to Des Moines. Five minutes later Donald's chasing me down the sand, snapping my behind with my wet towel. Rob excuses himself to return the Coke bottles to the refreshment stand for the deposit he didn't pay.

Weeks later I get a letter post-marked Des Moines.

Dear Margo, the name's Rob Faulkner. Means nothing to you at present but read on. You may recall a day in late August when an uncouth slob named Donald Allan attempted to pick you up on the sunny shores of Bradford Beach. Donald was the creep who spilled Coke on your *Photoplay*, kicked sand into your fries, and burnt a hole in your beach towel in his valiant effort to make a lasting impression.

The quiet, tanned, handsome fellow in the white swim suit was, of course, me. Though we never spoke, I'm hoping you may still have a faint memory of the boy who at least did not add to the calamity of your day.

I do read on. Miss Zeller praised me for writing like Virginia Woolf; but I don't want to write like Woolf anymore, I want to write like Rob Faulkner—with irony, vanity, and wit. Though I don't dot my *i*'s with balloons or sign my name with a smiley-face, I do burden my prose with exclamation points and italics. I respond viscerally to Rob's cool style. At the same time I distrust it.

His letter of September 15 begins a correspondence. Soon I wait for a letter in my box with the suspense I waited for Emma to stop raving or the next James Mason movie. By November he's invited me to Des Moines for the Christmas holidays.

Then one day after algebra, Vera informs me I have a visitor in the lounge.

Donald Allan is staring out a window, trench coat collar up, fedora down, unlit cigarette dangling from his lower lip.

"Let's b-blow this dump."

The neighborhood bristles with eyes: Milwaukee Downer College, Hartford Elementary, Milwaukee University School, Milwaukee Teachers College, Downer Sem. The enemy can pop up anywhere. I thrust my cigarette farther up my sleeve.

"I got a w-wire shoved through my head when I was ten."

"A *wire,* Donald?"

"Yeath. Haven't been able to think s-straight ever since."

"How awful."

"Know something? I've been kicked out of six schoolth."

"Congratulations."

He takes his cigarette out of his mouth and hits me on the back. "Ha, ha! Congratulathions. That's g-good!"

From that moment Donald MacIvor Allen becomes my devoted slave. Every day after class I find a blue slip in my box announcing a phone call or a visitor in the lounge. I try, but I fail to discourage him.

"Who's the cute boyfriend?"

"Oh," I say desperately, unwilling to admit the village idiot is after me, "that's 'T.R.'."

"'*T. R.*'?"

I have no idea what "T.R." stands for.

"Yeah, T. R. The, the—*The Raper.*"

Some girls start giving little shrieks when Donald stalks into the lounge, hands thrust deep into raincoat pockets.

"Oh, T.R. You scare me to death!"

"What's thith 'T.R.' bit?" he asks me with blue-eyed innocence.

"Your nickname. You'll never guess." I widen my eyes. "*The Raper*!"

He tilts his head sideways, a signal he's trying to think.

"Ha, ha! The Raper. That's g-good."

I meet his family. His sister Patsy really did go to Downer because there's her photo on the grand piano. Like all Downer graduates, she is tilting into the frame at a softly-lit sixty-degree angle, virginal white organdy ruff foaming about bare shoulders. Donald's younger sister Jean is all fun and freckles, with a lisp like Donald's.

"I'm drinking rum and coke." She swaggers.

"Aren't you a tad young?"

"Nexth year I graduate from Lower Thcool into ninth." She winks. "Good times are gonna roll!"

Mrs. Allan is narrow and elegant, brown hair swept up in a halo of crisp curls from her handsome, bony face. She's Downer's chaperone of choice because she calls for girls in a staid Lincoln, abandons them to a night of mayhem, promptly retrieves them for check-in. Patricia Allen is cool, ironic, and currently on her third scotch.

Mr. Allan terrifies me. Like his wife, he is tall and narrow; he wears a dark business suit, white shirt, and tartan tie. He holds his body tilted forward, like a man with a gale at his back. He has immaculately combed sandy hair and light eyelashes shading cold, bleached eyes. He can't take them off me.

"Scotch?"

I want to live up to the sophistication, but I loathe scotch.

"Could I maybe have a whiskey sour?"

When he throws open the doors of his cavernous liquor cabinet I realize I can have any intoxicant in the world.

He hands me a drink, clasps his hands behind his back like a schoolmaster. "You're a McCullough. What are your Scottish antecedents?"

I go cold. Long ago I decided I'm a McCullough ("I married him for his name") not a Merkel. Yet I know nothing about my father's family and am too ashamed to admit to this snob that my parents are divorced.

"Do the McCulloughs have a castle in Scotland?"

"C'mon, D-dad!" Donald is trying to save me.

"Five or six," I laugh. According to Emma, my father's family were horse thieves or Jews or worse.

He splashes himself another Johnny Walker Black.

"Edzell Castle is the seat of the Allan clan."

"Wow," I say inadequately.

"Mary, Queen of Scots stayed at Edzell and the castle was visited twice by James the Sixth."

Dumb with ignorance, I squirm under his stare.

"Look at them, Patricia—they even *look* alike, Margo and Donald. Same blue eyes, same black eyelashes, same short nose."

I look at Donald. It's true. He could be my brother.

Mr. Allan lifts his glass to us.

"I intend that my only son and his bride will reclaim Edzell Castle."

These are not Emma's wild rants, but I recognize madness in his pale eyes.

A maid announces dinner.

We're on a school bus driving twenty-five miles west to St. John's Military Academy in Delafield for a dinner dance. Raucous with anticipation, we shout away the miles:

I go to Downer Sem so pity me,
There ain't a damn man in this nunnery.
And every night at eight they lock the door,
I don't know what the hell I ever went here for!
And when I'm on that train and homeward bound,
I'm going to turn that home town upside down:
I'm going to smoke and drink and neck and pet
For what the heck: To hell with Downer Sem!

Or St. John's own anthem:

You can tell, by the smell
That your sister isn't well
When her time of the month's
Come around—

I turn around and there's our chaperone Miss Erbe ripping along with us.

Shrieks at the Red Circle Inn, a sign St. John's is near. Sporting St. John's pins on cashmere sweaters, most girls have boyfriends to meet them. My freshman buddy Sandy Jones and I eye each other nervously and wonder if we'll be wall flowers all night.

Passing a small lake, we turn into a long driveway punctuated by cannons poking stiffly at the sky, stone buildings more ultra-Gothic than Downer's brick. The bus brakes into a posse of milling cadets.

I have no memory of meeting Lt. Jack Reed—only of his powerful physical presence as we slow-dance to my favorite song "Secrets, whispered in the dark last night." He's about four inches taller than my five-six, with broad shoulders and narrow hips. He glides rather than walks, tucking his bum under so that his pelvis thrusts forward. His thick, military-cut blond hair is furrowed by wet comb marks. He doesn't say much, but his warm hand exploring my back tells me all I need to know. I've never met anyone so dangerously beautiful. In a trance I ride the bus back to Downer dated up for our Christmas dance and any time he can get leave.

At the same time I'm opening letters from Ben X, who has forgiven me for prom. Since there's no danger of anyone from Downer meeting him, I cut out a red heart, paste a photo of East Hill heartthrob Richie Stevens in the middle, label it "Ben" and add him to my bulletin board. I'm dizzy with boys, I feel popular at last—almost as popular as beautiful Emma or heart-smasher Elsie. Yet I can't help thinking about that visit to Des Moines:

> Dear Rob: Thank you for another of your amusing, witty letters! My mother isn't sure whether your parents want me to come to Des Moines, or only you. Somehow she doesn't seem to think that five minutes on Bradford Beach constitutes enough of an acquaintance for a visit. Maybe if your mother wrote to my mother, she'd let me come.
>
> Last night Donald called and asked me to the movies. I refused, but then *Mrs. Allan* called and asked. Donald must have had a knife in her back. So we're going to SORRY, WRONG NUMBER tomorrow night. Don't think me too horrible.
>
> Tell your mother to write mine! love, Margo

No question of Elsie "letting me come," she's delighted. The problem is calculating the hell Emma can create and, since Marie will be paying for my plane ticket, winning her support for the trip. Mrs. Faulkner does write Elsie; Elsie writes back "Yes!" So much for me playing hard to get. I'll fly from Wausau to Des Moines two days after Christmas.

My formal for the Christmas dance, courtesy of Marie from Emma Lange's, one of Milwaukee's snazziest stores, is a dreamy white strapless creation with a floating skirt and a bodice studded with rhinestones like ice over snow. During the fifth dance, Jack pins his St. John's insignia above my heart, folds me in his arms, and glides me around the floor cheek to cheek. My knees wobble with desire, I know I'm in love, I *want* to be in love, a love set to our favorite song "Many a tear has to fall, but it's all in the game. . . . ." Jack and I kiss all night. Miss Zeller has to tear us apart at the door.

December 21 I'm home. Elsie meets me with a wink for my coming Des Moines adventure. Strangely enough, Marie's happy for me too, perhaps because the Faulkners are friends of the Allans, a "Downer family." Johnny won't be told until the last minute: he's unpredictable about any activity he can't boss. Grandfather? No one ever tells poor Grandfather anything.

In the kitchen Emma is burning mince pies.

"Hi, I'm home. Shouldn't those pies come out of the oven?"

"Don't teach your grandmother how to suck eggs!"

All is calm, all is bright.

Next morning I beat Emma to the mailbox, whipping a letter from Des Moines out of Mr. Close's frozen mitten:

> What is this horrible news? When I came home yesterday there was that awful letter from your mother sending your regrets....
>
> Just because your uncle is coming to Wausau why does that mean you can't come here? Won't you please reconsider. We really should have a few days together to get acquainted, you know. It's hard, realizing that you know that fiend Donald better than you know me. My father, mother, and sister, not to mention myself, were looking forward to your visit. If you don't come we shall be crushed.
>
> Please persuade your mother to alter her decision. Or is it really yours?
>
> Disappointed in Des Moines......

I throw on my coat and run all the way to the *Record-Herald* building bursting in on my mother in her Society Editor office. She's lighting one Pall Mall on the butt of another.

"How could you!"

But as she scans the letter, I know.

"*Emma.*"

"Oh, Honey!"

"*What am I going to do?*"

"It's too late now."

"No it's not!"

These are the Glory Days of the US Post Office when a letter is delivered next day anywhere in the United States for three cents. I write the Faulkners: there's been a mix-up, I can come after all. Now I only have to live through the hours until five p.m. December 27, when I try to leave Emma's house for the Wausau airport.

Innocent, respectable, and sane in Des Moines, the Faulkners unknowingly poison our Christmas. Emma may not know I'm leaving the 27th, but she can't forget that a strange male has dared invite me to his home.

"Picked him up *on the beach, scheisse*-hoor, Can't wait to crawl into his bed! Or are you going all that way for his daddy?"

I want to vomit, I want to cry. But this time I'm also furious. The thought that Emma may be trying to protect me in her own crazed way from sex and pregnancy never occurs to me, nor does the possibility that she has reason to distrust Elsie and Marie's judgment of my emotional maturity. I only know I hate her.

"*If she tries to stop me I'll kill her.*" There, said at last.

The only plane in the world for Des Moines leaves at 5 p.m., with a stop in Milwaukee on the way. I've never flown before and it has to be at night.

Emma shatters the dawn before breakfast. I hide my suitcase under a quilt in my closet and go for a walk—anything to kill time. The day drags on, I drift downtown to the library where, at age twelve, I began my project of reading every book on the shelves in alphabetical order, a project abandoned a year later when I'd not only read a truly disgusting number of bad books but hadn't even gotten halfway through the *A*s. Johnny of the flaring temper and strength to stop me from leaving now worries me more than Emma.

At three I sneak in the side door. Nervous as a bat in daylight, Marie tells me that she called the taxi this morning and that Johnny's out running errands. Grandfather's playing cards at the Eagles. In the kitchen Emma's turning the Christmas turkey into some weird gumbo to go over rice. The plan is for Marie to divert Emma in the kitchen while Elsie gets me and my suitcase out the front door. At four p.m. I creep downstairs wearing my new bedroom slippers to muffle my footsteps. As I cross the front room Marie's voice rises hysterically in the kitchen:

"Now, Mother, you've no right to say such things about Margo—"

Emma's not been fooled by Marie's clumsy subterfuge; anyway, she's always been psychic when it comes to our trying to escape. She bursts through the kitchen door, filthy apron strained across her big stomach. I see again that her hands, arms and shoulders are powerful.

"Where you think *you're* going, my fine lady!"

"Now, Mother—"

With one furious swipe Emma knocks tall, weedy Marie to the floor.

"What's going on here?" Johnny's entrance is quiet, his voice tensely calm.

"Your hooring niece—!"

He puts his arm around Emma and winks at me. "Your cab's waiting, Margo."

Teeth chattering, Elsie holds open the front door.

I run. I leave them to their fates.

I refuse to care. I'm young, I'm headstrong, and not even Emma Merkel is going to stop me from pursuing this adventure.

If the Faulkners find it bizarre that I'm wearing bedroom slippers when I take off my boots, they don't say so. In Des Moines, at the party Rob throws for me in their newly painted recreation room, I pick up two more admirers, who deluge me with letters and threaten to land their private plane on Downer's hockey field. I don't believe a word they say; still, two more trophy photos go up on the bulletin board. Rob doesn't seem to mind, happy the party went off with a bang. I am possessed, dizzy—up to my neck in boyfriends. I play the pop hit "I Remember the Cornfields" until I have to tape the center hole of the record to keep it from skidding on the turntable. The song reminds me of Rob. "Sometimes I almost wish you hadn't come," he writes, "it feels so awful now you've left." We're already planning my visit to his family's cottage at Lake Delavan when school gets out in June. One old love is out of my life. James Mason in California sunshine is not my hero of British fogs: he's moved to Hollywood and making *awful* films like *Caught.*

Three days after I return to Downer Vera hands me a different kind of note:

> Will you please see me in my office promptly at
> four o'clock this Thursday.
> Yours sincerely,
> NAR WARREN TAYLOR

CHAPTER TWENTY-TWO

I expect a dungeon furnished with sinister black leather and blood-red draperies, behind which rot the bones of recalcitrant students like me. Gargoyles as well, and the rack and an iron maiden or two. Had she met my expectations, I might have flung myself on the carpet and worshipped her.

I stand. Her ho-hum office is hung with ordinary floral drapes drawn back from windows that cheerfully overlook the familiar front lawn. Miss Taylor sits behind an ordinary desk.

That stops me on the carpet. She is not ordinary, sitting tall and cool, a paisley scarf looped round her neck, dimples punctuating her cheeks but her jaw tight. I don't reason that as a first-year headmistress she too may be feeling strain. I just register again the visceral dislike I'd felt the first day Nar Warren Taylor took Chapel.

"Ah hope you had a lovely Christmas vacation?"

"Lovely," I say cautiously.

"And that you are all bright and eagah for the new term."

"Yes, Ma'am."

She flaps some papers at me, frowns.

"I have your teachers' reports here, Margo, and I'm sorry to say they are disappointing."

"Oh?"

"Particularly for a scholarship student."

"Oh."

"Mademoiselle says you should be getting an *A* but that your verb tenses are appallingly careless."

True.

"Miss Haney says that your preparation for biology is non-existent and your interest in the subject nil."

True.

"Miss Main writes that you are struggling with the most basic principles of algebra."

Bingo.

I lean forward in my chair. "But what does Miss Zeller say?"

Miss Taylor frowns at another document.

"'Margo's exceptional ability both to create and appreciate poetry has been evidenced during this goal period. I hope she will soon discover, however, that no amount of imaginative sympathy for poetry will suffice unless that sympathy is accompanied by *study*.'"

Unmasked again.

She shakes her auburn head gravely, opens another folder and recoils as though it's the most damning of all. A vase of white and red chrysanthemums left over from the Junior-Senior hockey game celebration stands near her elbow. Their petals are turning brown, they smell rotten.

"I am also more than alarmed by your Dormitory Citizenship Record. Mrs. Holmes has rated you "Good" in several categories, but—I am sorry to say—never 'Excellent.'" She leans back and draws a breath. "And for a scholarship student to earn only "Fair" for care of room, attending promptly to tasks, and awareness of opportunities to be helpful is a disgrace. And to receive 'Poo-ah' in 'maintenance of intelligent, constructive attitudes' is, frankly, unacceptable."

I hang my head. She pushes a box of tissues toward me across her big desk. I'm not crying.

A clock ticks in the silence. Out of nowhere it occurs to me that since Downer my hand-writing has changed from a swift forward script to writing that tilts acutely backward, as though blown by a stiff east wind. *Why?*

"Of course my real reason for calling you in today is less to chastise you for last semester's mediocre performance than to encourage you to improve this term. I'm sure that with effort you *will* improve."

I brighten. "Especially since this semester I won't have algebra, and I'll have Madame for English."

Dimples again, still no smile. "There will be other courses just as challenging as algebra, Margo. The classes are not the problem, your poo-ah study habits are. Will you promise me to work hard on improving them?"

"Yes, Miss Taylor."

I leave her office red as the Downer crest but, alas, with no deep sense of sin. I've missed my hot-fudge sundae at the drugstore with Robin and Sandy. I don't regret missing (a note in my box informs me) the call in person of Donald Allan.

When Elsie receives Mrs. Holmes's report, she scribbles across the top "Ten *Goods*—hurrah!" O god, she's telling everybody that I'm doing brilliantly at Milwaukee Downer because she needs so badly to believe it.

Emma seems to have repented her Christmas violence, writing me this semester short vivid letters: "It snowed a bushel-basket this morning" . . . . "There's a big fat jay skating on the birdbath" . . . . "Last night the wind almost howled the house down" . . . . "Today I spied three darling crocuses uncovering their purple heads . . . Apple blossoms wait your return."

Why am I surprised? This was the girl who wrote poetry secretly at night under the bedcovers, the word-hungry woman who possibly passed on to me whatever writing ability I possess.

She also sends packages of "treats."

"It's not food," I insist, shaking the box addressed in Emma's slashing hand. "I can tell."

Girls crowd round.

"Pig! Selfish! Look, it says *'Perishable.'*"

Tearing off wrappings, they find Emma's "fruit bars": yellow squares of desert-dry sponge cake studded with a few carelessly chopped dates. Sandy spits hers into her hand.

"*They're from our maid,*" I say desperately—"*and our maid can't cook.*"

Emma encloses a note with the disaster. "Margo, I'm so happy you're going to such a fine school, *with no bad boys*, and I know you'll bring poor Marie great credit."

This sobers me like nothing else. Thinking of Marie slaving away at Milwaukee Teachers College to pay for my tuition and boarding fees and all the extras, not to mention Elsie in Wausau scratching up five dollars a month toward my charged Downer clothes, I really do try harder this semester.

Geometry makes an aesthetic sense that algebra totally lacked; also geometry isn't taught by Massachusetts Main. Unlike young Miss Zeller, Madame Van Wagenen presides with humor and irony over a relaxed English class. Cheery, muscular Mrs. Weigel, our gym teacher, lets me substitute ice skating for the basketball I loathe. I assure stubby, brown Miss Haney that I find dissecting earthworms fascinating.

But I'm crazy with undefined longings, I can't settle down. "I feel as though there are prison bars on these windows," I write Rob with breathtaking originality. We're bussed to Northwestern Naval Academy on the shores of Lake Geneva where I meet Joshua Pericles Sandos, exchange farewell kisses, pin another photo on my burdened bulletin board. Donald calls daily. Dangerous Jack Reed takes me out any weekend he can get a furlough. One of these weekends he almost talks me into sneaking up the back stairs while he books himself into the Astor Hotel. We're standing on Wisconsin Avenue in front of the hotel holding hands, a frigid Lake Michigan wind blasting up Milwaukee's main drag. Somehow I find the wits to say no. "Jack, we can't. If we're caught we'll both be expelled."

Yet I'm so obsessed with conquering I can't even leave Marie's boyfriend alone.

She has been dating a man named Pickens Johnson. One Thursday night she invites us both to a little candlelight supper at Shepherd House, the dorm she's house-mothering for MTC. Marie cooks strictly from cans, but in these days canned tuna, mushrooms, and cream of chicken soup with a crushed potato-chip topping passes for gourmet. Pickens eats with reasonable appetite as I flirt tentatively with him across the table. He's an executive (I think) with Allis Chalmers—tall and lean with a face that is all planes and angles and a pale complexion: Leslie Howard with prematurely white hair. He wears a grey tweed suit with a dark blue shirt, silk ascot, and (I glance under the table) immaculately polished mahogany-brown loafers.

I am smitten.

Leaning toward Marie to indicate he considers my fluttering eyelashes a bore, he chats easily in a cultivated voice with just a hint of Virginia accent—so different from Nar Warren's drawl. I listen, chin in hand, worshipping. Marie excuses herself to get dessert and coffee.

"Pickens, may I call you Pickens?"

He lowers his fork, politely turns to me. "Yes, of course."

"I have a ton of homework tonight so I really have to leave soon. Could you possibly drive me back to the Sem?" I have *nothing* in mind, I just long to be alone for a few minutes with an apparently normal, rational adult.

Marie returns with pineapple upside-down cake and Nescafe.

Pickens checks his watch. "Of course I can drive you back. But let's have dessert first. Then I think your aunt looks as though she'd like a little outing."

Because he seems immune to my charms, pathetic as they are, Marie allows me to be included in his invitation to dinner a week later at his Downer Avenue apartment a few blocks north of the Sem. But she recoils when I teeter in on heels, wearing the black and gold lamé party dress with the plunging neckline she bought me last December for a Downer dance. My lashes are stiff with Maybelline, I reek of Evening in Paris, my preposterously long rhinestone earrings nip my shoulders.

Marie's wearing a twin sweater-set and a plain wool plaid skirt, Pickens grey slacks, a navy v-neck pullover, and those mahogany tasseled loafers.

"To what," says Pickens raising his eyebrows with his glass of wine, "do we owe this splendor?"

This time he notices. Marie seethes. I scintillate—or think I do—trotting out the dazzling sophistication of a Downer sophomore who's just read *Les Miserables* and *Hamlet* for the first time. After a dinner stiff with her resentment, Marie scrapes back her chair to carry dishes into Pickens' kitchen. When she comes back for the salad plates I'm sitting on his lap.

She goes white.

"Pickens, this is monstrous! Margo, how can you behave in this appalling manner!"

Pickens lowers his long legs and I slide off.

"Now, Marie, this is just a kid. Your niece, for god's sake. She's been telling me how much she's always missed having a father."

"You expect me to believe you're being *fatherly*?" Marie stalks to the bedroom and returns with her coat, yanks it our of his hands when he attempts to hold it for her. "I insist you drive me home immediately. Margo can damn well walk!"

"Look here." Pickens' face is crimson, his aplomb shattered. "We haven't had coffee and dessert. I bought your favorite strawberry schaum torte, I have some excellent brandy—"

"You think schaum torte matters, after this—*outrage!*"

As Emma always says, poor Marie. I don't think she's had a serious boyfriend since Louis back in the 1930's.

"Good bye, Pickens. I'm so sorry."

He shakes his head in distress, loathing the scene. And with that gesture I know Marie's blown it with Pickens as she did with Louis.

And that it's entirely my fault.

Back in the dorm I am sickened and ashamed. I finger-strip the disgusting tar from my eyelashes, race down the hall to the bathroom, and punish my face with a scrub brush. I kick the black and gold lamé into my closet. I'll never wear it again.

Yet in bed, miserable and furious at myself, I'm overtaken by rebellious thoughts. *Marie deserves it, doesn't she?* Always rooting me out of my secret places. Always "Now we must be up and doing." Always thrusting a broom into my hand. Always shoving me into a chair to write thank you notes or do the family mending. Not to mention that I'm furious at her stupidity over this Pickens thing. I *am* just a kid, her niece. *I'm family*. She should have laughed at me.

She never lets me see Pickens again. I can't blame her. Of course any weekend I choose I can stroll three blocks up Downer to his apartment and ply my juvenile charms.

I don't.

The Pickens disaster does not prevent Marie from rescuing me from spending Easter vacation in Wausau, which, after Thanksgiving and Christmas, I dread so deeply I've been coaxing Jack Reed to run away with me rather than my going home. Marie tells me she's been hired to keep an eye on a mansion overlooking Lake Michigan that MTC recently purchased for a new dorm.

"I actually have permission for you and a friend to stay at Lakeshore Dorm during spring vacation. Why not ask Mary Connor? She seems like an intelligent person. I understand her parents practically *own* the north woods."

Mary is tall, overweight, and sardonic, with enormous, gelatinous, grey-blue eyes. She's always brushing her teeth in the second-floor bathroom. I love her. She wears plain blouses and skirts, no jewelry. I've never given her parents' bank account a thought.

"Can you stay over?"

"Quel panique," says Mary.

We choose a big double room on the second floor overlooking the lake. The lower floor is under construction: tools, coiled wires, plaster dust and wheelbarrows of cement stand around under tarps. We don't mind.

That Friday night we have dates with college boys. Subsequent trauma has obliterated their names from memory. Pity, because we all had a fine time: dropping into an Episcopalian Good-Friday service to sing at the top of our lungs, playing hide and seek in Lake Shore Park, rocking with laughter over hamburgers in a White Castle booth. They escort us back to Lake Shore Dorm, kiss us good night with gentlemanly restraint, promise to call for us tomorrow.

"Weren't they *lovely*."

"Dreamy."

"So polite—I don't mean *geeky*, just *civilized*."

"Exactly. How often does one meet *civilized?*"

Next morning pounding on the front door wakes me. Mary moans, turns over in her bed. I squint at my watch: seven-thirty.

We'd gone to bed at two. What the heck! I throw on my robe, run downstairs.

"*Come with me.*"

"Why?"

"Mary too."

"*What?*"

"Never mind, I've got something to show you."

I call up to Mary. She staggers down in robe and slippers, rolling big blue eyes.

We march after Marie across the foyer, sidestepping planks and power drills. She stops at a small door, throws it open, points.

We stare into a bathroom, tiles stacked in the tub, plaster in the sink.

"So?"

The finger jerks spasmodically.

"*The toilet seat is up.*"

Mary and I look at each other blankly.

"How do you explain your conduct, Margo, after I *trusted* you and went out of my way to accommodate you and Mary!"

"*What are you talking about!*" I mutter, paralyzed with shock and apprehension.

"I expressly forbade you to have men in this house while you were staying here. Obviously men *are* in this house. I'm searching your rooms right now!"

I find voice. "Marie, *this is crazy!* "

"It is not crazy to be outraged at your appalling lack of consideration and judgment. I'll have to report you to the college authorities."

"We've done nothing wrong!"

"*The toilet seat is up.*"

To her chagrin she finds no men under our beds.

"I'm out of here," says Connor under her breath, tossing clothes into her suitcase. "I'm downtown and waiting for a bus."

"I'll go with you, Connor."

"You're not going anywhere, Margo. Monday morning you will meet with the Dean of our College."

I can not look Mary in the face to say goodbye.

That night Elsie calls in tears:

"What a ghastly way to treat Marie after all her kindness to you!"

"I have done nothing!"

"Now she'll absolutely *not* let you stay at her apartment before you visit Rob, in fact she says Delavan is out of the question. How *could* you!"

"We did not let boys into the dorm. *I* don't know why the toilet seat was up."

"She said they stayed the night."

I take a deep breath. "Believe me. They did not stay all night, they never got past the front door. Marie's more obsessed with sex than Grandmother. Tell her so for me!"

Monday morning I drag myself to Marie's college for a meeting with Charlotte Wollager, Dean of Students. Miss Wollager's ash-brown hair is clipped short; she wears a well-tailored suit with authoritative shoulder pads. I glance into Marie's office; she is looking injured and doodling with a pen. Eventually she joins us.

"Good morning, Margo. Have a chair. Your aunt has filled me in on what happened at Lake Shore Dorm last Friday night."

"Nothing happened, Dr. Wollager."

She smiles competently.

A man in overalls shuffles in the doorway.

"Come in, Mr. Laski. I thought"—she sweeps us with a bright glance—"we should have another witness in the case, as it were. Mr. Laski, can you tell us anything about this mysterious toilet seat?"

Marie shudders fastidiously.

"Nothing mysterious about it. Me and my men been working at Lake Dorm couple weeks now. We use the can off the front hall. Hope it ain't against no law."

"Not that I know of. And conceivably"—Dean Wollager is as calm as though discussing the price of cheese—"you might leave the toilet seat up after use?"

He scratches his head at the word "conceivably," but soldiers on.

"No law 'gainst that neither."

"You worked all day Friday."

"All day. Quit at five."

"Thank you, Mr. Laski. I think that clears up the situation."

I shake hands with Dr. Wollager, glare at wilted Marie, storm back to the Sem. Marie calls half an hour later.

"If you'd like to stay in my apartment the rest of spring vacation—"

"No, thank you, Marie. And you owe Mary Connor a written apology."

That afternoon the ancient Nurse Cora McAdow checks me into the Infirmary with a temperature of 103. I spend the whole week propped against pillows, staring at rows of white beds that look like coffins, cursing Marie's puritanism.

I should be on my knees confessing my own crimes. I should be spending serious time figuring out why my life is always jumping the track.

CHAPTER TWENTY-THREE

Possessing an iron will and sixteen-year-old hormones, I do visit the Faulkners after all, taking the bus to Delavan Lake right after Sem gets out. Afterward I take the Greyhound bus to Wausau, drag myself up Washington Street at five in the evening.

Grandfather: "Well, well, look who's home."

Elsie: "Honey, what a marvelous time you must have had!"

Marie: "I hope you realize you have responsibilities this summer. Life is not all play."

Johnny: "Is this really Miss McCullough of Downer Seminary? How my favorite niece has changed!"

"Sunburned harlot! Elsie's crazy letting you run around the state like a tramp!"

> Nine almost perfect days [I write Rob]. Is it
> disgustingly selfish of me to wish we'd spent a little
> more time without Muriel, Carson, Pixie, Roger
> and Donald in attendance? And to wish that you
> would hug and kiss me very hard just *once* a year?
> But maybe then it would hurt more than it does now
> to say goodbye.

Again, thank you for a wonderful time. As I told
you one night: "You know I love you best."
You don't seem to know, but I do.

The ache of that parting never does heal, quite. Yet an invitation from Mary Connor gives me something else to think about. With "'my parents'" permission, they will pick me up in Wausau for two weeks at their cottage. "Your friendship has meant a great deal to Mary this year," writes her mother on monogramed stationery. "We look forward to having you with us at the lake."

"Of course you'll go," says Emma, licking her lips. "*I* know Connors because they know Alexanders, they're big lumber too. Must be Plum Lake, like Judd. Look, I've found a pattern. I'll run you up a few pairs of shorts on the machine."

"The Connors aren't on Plum Lake and I don't need shorts, thank you, Grandmother."

"What if they want to come in?" Marie knots her hands.

"Why would they? There are few attractions."

"Mrs. Connor might have to use the—facilities."

"With the toilet seat up." A bitter thrust. Truly I shudder at the thought of any Connor using our only bathroom.

"I know," says Elsie. "Tell them you'll take the bus to Rhinelander, much more convenient. They can meet you there."

"But the Connors are going to be in Wausau that day anyway."

"Let them pick you up at the Hotel Wausau," says Emma surprisingly.

"What reason can I give?"

"Downtown. Save 'em trouble. Easy to find."

I sigh. None of this mattered at Downer. Mary was just a big good-natured pal with bad breath and a sarcastic sense of humor.

"I'll wait for them outside. They won't even get out of the car, I'll just hop in and we'll be off. Nobody has to *meet* them," I add threateningly.

"What if it's raining?" says Elsie bleakly.

"Let's not turn this into World War Two, okay?"

But my heart sinks as I wait on the sidewalk. Though my back is to 1016, I see it plainly: crouched between terraces, cramped, neglected and unlovely—on its knees begging for a new coat of paint, its snowball bushes trimmed, its grass edged. I don't know what the Connor place looks like, but if they're chums of the Alexanders, I know what it doesn't.

Why do I always put myself into a false position so that I'm always ashamed?

Mary's lip curls as she looks past my shoulder, but thank god nobody's got to go to the bathroom.

"Not *my* house," I say desperately, "I'm visiting my grandmother."

I can't tell if anyone believes me.

The Connor car purrs away the miles. I've never ridden in a Cadillac before, never seen such elegant-grey upholstery, such exquisite tortoise-shell ashtrays, such floor rugs thick as turf. Finally I see out the window that magical mix of maple, pine, birch and balsam that means the North Woods.

"Ladies, how about lunch?"

We're the only customers in the knotty-pine restaurant where glassy-eyed deer, elk, moose and bear stare down at me. They know I've no right here.

"Grilled cheese, please."

"Oh, no, Margo. We're having lobster."

Two waitresses bring in enormous silver dishes on legs so that burning candles can be slid under them to keep the lobsters warm. Other silver dishes over flames hold melted butter. *In my entire life I've never ever eaten anything more delicious.* And this is only lunch.

"Almost there," drawls Mary an hour and a half later. Mary is cool, never gets excited about anything. *My* heart is racing.

The next town is theirs, a wide main street right out of a Hollywood western.

"Got a few errands to do. Show Margo around, Mary."

Connor Hardware, Connor Lumber. Do they own the whole town?

"Everybody set for the island?" Mrs. Connor deposits armfuls of grocery bags in the trunk.

Island.

We drive to the shores of a large rippling dark-blue lake. At a dock a Chris-Craft rocks richly at anchor. We pile out of the Cadillac. I watch them load supplies into the boat. Mr. Connor takes my cheap suitcase, tucks it securely under the back seat. The motor roars.

"What's the name of the lake?" I ask Mary as we speed away.

"I *told* you, silly. We live on Birch Lake."

"You didn't mention lake," I say faintly.

A woman in a maid's uniform is standing on a dock to greet us. She finds the suitcase I'm trying to hide and lifts it out of my hand.

"This is our anchor and rudder," says Mrs. Connor, without naming the maid.

Mrs. Connor is much prettier than Mary, trim and chic, with big brown eyes and thick dark-blonde hair. She's wearing a white silk shirt open at her tanned throat, beautifully draped slacks, and white leather moccasins sewn with tiny red and black beads. Mr. Connor is an ordinary-looking man in a plaid shirt and chinos, stocky, balding. Mary walks ahead laughing, her arm around the maid's waist. I bring up the rear.

The lodge, set in a clearing of pine, oak and birch, is everything I've always dreamed a North Woods home could be. Mellow pine walls, beamed ceilings, fireplaces, low sofas in hunter-green plaid, long refectory table, windows everywhere inviting woods and water to step inside.

For the very first time I understand Emma; and Elsie, who ruthlessly corrects my English; and Marie, tutoring wealthy pupils; and Johnny running after the rich. Why not? Here is everything I've always longed for: elegance, solitude, privacy, beauty. What our family lusts for is right and good. We don't want power, global influence, flashy cars, corruption, political clout, tax-havens, trophy wives, billions. Just this. Has any of us realized that without money we don't stand a chance in hell of getting it? I don't think it's quite filtered through our noble but thick heads.

That night I'm awakened by eerie laughter volleying back and forth across the black lake. I shiver. What can it be? Tears burn my eyes. I bury my head in strange rough pillows, choke back my sobs.

Not a popular student at school, Mary is in her element at Birch Lake. She handles the speed boat, dives, swims a powerful crawl, paddles a canoe, hits bullseyes with bow and arrow, executes figure-eights on water skis. She can reel in walleye and pike, whack off their heads, gut them, scrape scales like confetti, thread them onto green sticks, broil them over the campfire she has made. When I try to describe the wild night music, she laughs.

"Stupido! Never heard a loon before?"

Then comes the day Mrs. Connor says, "Tennis anyone?"

By heart I know Johnny's lecture. "To Fit In With The Important People there are three sports you must know: swimming, riding, tennis." I have mastered the backstroke, I can (usually) stay on a horse, but no matter how many lessons Johnny's given me, a winning tennis stroke eludes me. Still, I brought my Wilson racket and a white sharkskin tennis outfit because, one fatal day at Downer when Mary asked me whether I played tennis, I'd said—like the idiot who doesn't realize tomorrow always comes: "Of course."

Their tennis court is on the mainland near their pier. Oh, maybe it isn't their private court, maybe other people use it; but everything seems to belong to them. It's Mary and her dad against Mrs. Connor and me. My knees are knocking. Mary smashes a hard ball at me, I chop it into the net: fifteen-love. By forty-love the Connors have taken my measure and Mrs. Connor is covering our side of the court, calling sportily, "I'll get this one!"

My playing goes downhill. Pretty soon Mr. Connor's mopping his brow, "By George, it's a hot one, one more game."

One more game.

Opposition serving, Mrs. Connor and I down forty-thirty, Mrs. Connor returns Mary's backhand and Mary nets the ball. Deuce. Mr. Connor tosses the ball and blasts a serve cross court. I see the ball barreling at me, close my eyes, and swing.

"Jolly good shot!" Mrs. Connor claps me on the back. I open my eyes. Mary's loping into a corner after the ball.

"Good work," says Mr. Connor kindly after Mrs. Connor wraps it up for us. Two miserable hours redeemed. I can breathe.

In town we stock up on groceries at the Connor Super Mart and make wake back to the island. Mr. Connor hitches the boat to the dock and everybody gets out but me because I'm fumbling with my racket that's gotten wedged under my seat.

"Just drop the anchor over, Margo, will you?"

"Right."

I've completely forgotten Marie's warning about her permanently injuring her back while helping the Morganthaus move from Hawaii: *"Never touch anything belonging to the rich."*

I stand up, heave the anchor, stagger, drop it squarely onto my seat. The wood shatters. I drop spreading my tennis skirt over the wreckage.

"What's that?" calls Mrs. Connor over her shoulder.

"Nothing."

"Get a move on, Miggy," laughs Mary. When she feels affectionate she calls me Miggy. My throat spasms with fear.

Too busy damning my cowardice to hell, I can't swallow dinner. All I had to say is, "Sorry, I accidentally dropped the anchor on the seat." Mr. Lumber Baron would have sauntered out on the pier, pooh-poohed the damage, told me the boat's insured. Too late. Now I'm a criminal.

The setting sun slides up the birch trunks, gilding them pink. "Skinny dipping," cries Mary. I'm shivering. Plump girls like Mary never seem to feel the cold. I take time shedding my clothes. By the time we dive off the pier the boat's invisible in the dark.

Nothing's said at breakfast. Mr. Connor excuses himself, kisses Mrs. Connor on the cheek. Every morning he takes the boat to the mainland. I head for my room and lie on the bed the maid's already made, feeling a criminal for mussing it. A knock. Mary stands there, hands on hips.

"Dad says the seat's broken on the Chris Craft."

"Really?"

"Says you must have dropped the anchor on it. Did you?"

"Don't know."

"Oh, come on! *Did* you?"

"Yes."

Mary lofts her upper lip in the sneer I adore when she uses it on others.

"Well, stupido, why didn't you *say* so?"

Because, stupido, the north woods belongs to you. Because you drive your own Chrysler convertible. Because your mother, flashing check books and bank forms, announces, "I'm devoting my morning to desk work." Because I'm conscience-stricken at my deceit, and because conscience makes cowards of us all. Because, you cow, you just called me stupido for the tenth time: nine times too often, stupido.

"I don't know."

She laughs unpleasantly and leaves.

Three days later they drive me to the Rhinelander airport as scheduled. Flying home (courtesy Marie) I vow I'll never set foot in the north woods again.

This fall semester, courtesy Mary Connor, everybody at Downer will know that I live in a hovel, can't play tennis, and smash boats.

"Well, Madame Mazonga." Where does Emma get these names? "Your mother's being hauled to jail 'cause she can't fork over for your debts."

I'm lost in Mary Webb's romantic novel *Gone to Earth.*

"You'd better get off your big bazoo and get a job."

She is spooning ice cream out of a quart cardboard bucket with a wire handle, a smear of raspberry ripple decorating the end of her nose. *Her* bazoo is enormous. I glare at her. But I do slink to Winkelman's and am hired in Sportswear at forty-five cents an hour, every cent of which I return to Winkelman's when I buy a sweater or a skirt for Downer.

It's a Sunday in July and I'm rocking on the front porch, loathing the thought of Winkelman's next day and idly watching a maroon Mercury convertible crawl past our house for the third time. It reappears heading down, slows, vaults the curb and snuggles a bumper against an elm on the tree lawn. A tall solid fellow with a glowing sunburn gets out, moves toward our porch, hands in pockets.

Donald Allan.

I panic, thinking of the Allan house with its breakfast room and butler's pantry and dining room papered in Chinese gold, its vast, cold living room where Mr. Allan gets neighborhood kids high on his Scotch and gin. My pride has been ground to dust by the Connors. I am too pulverized to face an Allan.

But he stands shyly at the bottom step.

"H-hi!"

'Donald, what are you doing here?"

"De-decided to borrow Pat-thy's car."

All summer Donald's been writing me.

My Dearest Margo,

It's hard to say the things I want to say to you.
I still love you, and will do anything you ask of me.
You probably will say I am too emotional, but it
is the way I feel about you.

I'm sorry I didn't get a chance to have a real talk
with you, my fault because I wouldn't go with
you and Rob, but I knew Rob would tell you
what I said. I'm not ashamed of anything I told
Rob about you, I wish that I could have told you
but I just couldn't have put it into words.

Please believe I would, and will do anything
I can for you, and Please believe that I love you
very much.

Maybe before school starts if Rob can come up and stay at my house, and of course I want you too if we have any room, preferably I would have just you, but I have to repay Rob for his kindness to me.

School is awfully boring.

I'm sending you a sealed envelope of what I expect to be doing 10 years from now.

My best wishes and regards to your mother. I hope she is in good health.

Please write to me as soon as you can.

Well, Dearest, I have to close now.
Never forget that I love you, and that you will always be in my heart.

All my love and kisses, Your most humble Servant

Donald "T.R." Allan

We don't hug, we don't kiss, we never have. As with Mary Connor, I'm too busy anguishing over a rich friend finding me in squalor.

"Let's go downtown for a Coke!" I'm urgent, aware of Emma lurking in the kitchen.

He pulls out a handkerchief, wipes his sweating forehead.

"Sure, but thay, how about a g-glath of water? I'm dying."

"Stay there. Well, no, come sit on the porch. I'll be right back."

I open the screen door.

Emma.

"*Caller?*"

Oh, god.

"Donald Allan." I try to herd her back into the parlor but she stands firm so I babble, "His sisters go to Downer Sem, Marie knows them, old Milwaukee family, castle in Scotland, Donald's going into his father's engineering firm—"

Shoving me aside, she thrusts her head around the door. Donald's sprawled in the rocking chair, fanning his red face with the Sunday comics.

"Hello, young man!" Emma ripples seductively up and down the scale.

"H-hello."

"Bet you'd like a tall, cold glass of lemonade."

"Gosh, you bet!"

"I'm Margo's grandmother, Mrs. Merkel."

Donald rises to shake hands. She offers hers around the screen door which she holds in front of her stomach.

"It's a shame my daughters aren't here to welcome you, Mr. Allan. Well, I'm off to do the honors. You cool yourself in the rocker. Margo will keep you company."

When she returns with pitcher and glasses clinking on a tray, she's put on a clean apron and pinned up her unruly hair. She chants bewitchingly her old refrain:

"Ice cold lemonade
Made in the shade.
Frogs at the bottom
But don't be afraid!"

"I'm sure not afraid!"

"Margo, pull the table over near the door. I'd like to talk to this nice young man."

And there they sit, screen door between them, Emma a shadowy priestess in the confessional. He tells her he's been kicked out of six schools.

"My, my." She chuckles seductively. "They don't know a good man when they see one."

("You call yourself a *man* !")

Then she starts to re-live her life.

"Driving our cows home at twilight I expected Indians to leap from the forest, though never saw an Indian, except once when they came to our back door. You know Indian hair, straight as a horse tail, well, I had *curls* and all the men went crazy for 'em, Judd Alexander included. You know the Alexanders, fine people—"

"Grandmother, *please.*"

Donald is gallantly devouring sugar cookies burnt black around the edges. He wipes his mouth and stands up. "Margo, I got to get going."

"But you just got here."

"My thister doesn't know about her c-car."

"Such a long drive for so little."

He beams at me. "Hey, I thaw you again, didn't I? Wait'll I tell that dope Rob what he's missing. Can't believe that g-guy can't get on the ball. You've got a real nith place here. And your g-grandma's thwell."

"I'll write."

He tenderly punches my shoulder. "You d-damn well better."

After complicated minutes with clutch, hand brake and reverse, the Mercury convertible detaches itself from the tree, lurches over the curb, and roars down the hill.

Though it's only mid-July, to me it feels like the end of summer.

CHAPTER TWENTY-FOUR

"Hi, Mrs. Holmes, back again." As usual she's swigging Coke, forehead pleated in a frown. Downer again, junior year. Everything looks the same.

"So sorry, Margo," says Mrs. Holmes. "I realize she was your best friend."

"Who?"

"Mary Connor. Her parents have transferred her to Dana Hall in Massachusetts."

I laugh. So the Connors now judge Downer substandard because I go there? I laugh too because now Mary can't tell about the Wausau house. But upstairs in my room, tucking away panties, slips and sweaters in bureau drawers, I feel hollow as a cored apple. Then I discover that Robin Wrezin, my mate next door, hasn't returned—Robin of the boy-cut hair and mischievous eyes, in whose room I spent almost as much time as my own.

I really don't have other friends, except maybe Sandy Jones because she dates Gage Barker, Jack Reed's buddy.

Jane, Lynn, Marcia, yes—but they're all sophomores and again I feel I should be picking on someone my own size. The ache persists. I'm not elected to any office; schoolwork is endless and terrifying. Compared to the feats of girls like Betty, Beachy and Lolly, my total ineptness in gym class humiliates me. True to Emma's code, I gauge myself only by the stars. There must be run-of-the-mill girls at Downer; I never notice them.

Adrift, I become reckless. Miss Erbe, the music teacher, walks into the lounge where I'm at the grand playing Beethoven's "Pathetique Sonata."

"Why Margo, that's wonderful! I had no idea you could play."

"I can't."

"You, can! More than a little, my dear."

"Actually I just picked this up listening to the record by Arthur Rubinstein," I say insanely, repeating the theme in triplets. "It wasn't hard."

Miss Erbe's mouth drops agape.

"You mean you're playing the "Pathetique" simply from *hearing* it?"

Actually after seeing *The Seventh Veil* I'd run out and bought all the music Ann Todd plays in the film and I'd been working at the *Pathetique* slow movement ever since.

"Yes." Insane, insane.

"But that's incredible."

Totally.

That night in dining hall I see Erbe talking excitedly to her faculty table mates. Still, I have no real sense of doom when I walk into the lounge for music class next day, choose an inconspicuous corner, and open my notebook. Miss Erbe comes in a moment later, eyes glowing.

"Girls, we have a very special treat. Yesterday, I discovered that Margo has an incredible talent. She has actually learned how to play Beethoven's "Pathetique Sonata" just from *listening to a recording!* Isn't that amazing?" She opens the piano lid and beckons. "Margo, I hope you'll share your gift with us today."

All eyes are on me. *This cannot be happening.* Can I pretend to vomit, then run? An expectant hostility in the room tells me I don't dare. I rise, creep to the piano and drop onto the bench, praying for instant death. I poise my hands above the keys. Miss Erbe flashes me a proud smile.

I make it through the slow part, fingers like lead sinkers, yet so far so good. I simply can't tackle the place where Beethoven gets going. I close the lid.

"That should give you an idea," I mumble, sliding off the bench.

"Amazing," a senior hisses at me at the end of class, and I know not one of the girls believes I've just picked this sonata up from a record.

Today I look at my 1950 *Crest* yearbook, amazed at messages in fading Schaeffer blue ink: "Lots of Love," "Love ya," "Love to a wonderful sex box."

I do not feel loved. At sixteen I haven't a clue who I am; have no faith that I possess the slightest brains, abilities, or character. Drop into this void my turbulent mix-ups with boyfriends, the anarchy that's possessed me ever since Mother abdicated to "Elsie," my horror at having been sent to Downer in the first place—well, I can see clearly now that I doomed myself.

At the time I understand nothing. I'm crazy, driven by an irresistible urge to show off, break rules, flaunt traditions. Surely a psychiatrist today would immediately label my behavior a cry for help.

My transgressions are childish, yet since institutions function by rules, I realize now they disrupted school morale. As a sophomore I'd clocked in a few times after five, been campused once, earned perhaps half a dozen demerits—not good for a house officer, but not criminal either.

In my junior year I cut loose. I'm late for study and returning on weekends. I miss chapel. I violate lights out. My newest caper is leading midnight kitchen raids. If I really want to get expelled, all I'd have to do is smoke in my room; but—yipes—I don't want to be packed back to Emma either—though everything I do invites just that. As it is, I now smoke openly after school: on the street, in the drugstore, in the restaurant across Downer Avenue. I add more photos of males to my bulletin board. My grades are mediocre. I'm not even getting an *A* from my (rather less) adored Madame Van Wagenen.

Rob is my only confidant:

Just back now from Rockford and my new friend Sarah's house. When we stepped on that Peoria-bound train, Sarah and I really cut loose, beat three packs of weeds before I got deathly sick, though I did pull myself together enough to down a few Dacharies before the train pulled into the station.

We were met by a carload of kids and whisked off to Sarah's house where a big party was in full swing. First question I was asked, "Do you French kiss?" Naturally I felt I had to say yes. Then we all went swimming in her outdoor heated pool. Next day we bummed around in Sarah's convertible picking up boys. That night a barbeque.

Colored lights, soft music, handsome boys—what more could I ask for.

(You?)

Rob, I'm in a most *restless* mood. I can hardly wait to get out of school and get married. I want a house with forest green walls and thick white carpets. But all I really want is to get out of here. I suppose this sounds totally insane. And a zoology test tomorrow! Write the minute you get this.

Love and other indoor sports—

Rob advises restraint, but I'm beyond help. Besides, the delay between my "Write the minute you get this" and his rebukes, combined with his cool "We must get together sometime," chill me. So there will be no invitation to Des Moines this winter holiday. Never do I figure that my exaggerated accounts of my "sex life" might turn him off rather than on. Never do I figure anything. Emotions drive me like a gull in a storm. I haven't a clue how to control them. By the time I leave for Wausau on December 18, I've chalked up fifteen infractions and—unless I can miraculously ace semester exams in January—three *C*'s and two *B*'s. Keeping my scholarship means maintaining a *B* average.

Wausau is blanketed with the snow I used to love but which now seems like the death of my hopes. My bleak vacation I spend at the movies killing my teeth with Milk Duds while watching mediocre films like *In the Good Old Summertime, Fighting Man of the Plains,* and *Task Force.* Cheerlessly, I sit through James Mason in *East Side, West Side.* I hate Hollywood for turning him into a weakling, it, hate him more for letting it.

For Christmas, Emma gives everybody toys she's ordered from a Montgomery Ward catalogue. A doll stove for her husband. A collapsible donkey that brays when you pull a string for Johnny. For Elsie a bottle of glycerine and a bubble pipe. For Marie celluloid twin baby dolls in a cradle.

Emma watches me open a toy train. I know what this means. Rail Rider.

She doesn't seem to realize who has turned me into a regular on the Wausau-Milwaukee line.

I do not ace my January exams and am miles from feeling, in Nar Warren Taylor's words, "bright and eagah for the new term." I continue to check in late for five-fifteen study and forget to sign the off-campus book. One night in the subterranean dorm kitchen where three desperados are digging cherry ice cream out of an institution-sized tub with our fingers, the overhead light snaps on.

"Disgusting!" says Mrs. Holmes, lip knotting in contempt. "And you, Margo, five pounds overweight."

My criminal file bulges.

Jack Reed's friend Gage Barker has transferred his affections from Sandy Jones to Phoebe Stone. Since boys dictate girls' friendships, Phoebe and I are now friends. I'd have wanted her as a friend in any case. Phoebe is bright and funny, with shiny black bangs, small brown eyes, white skin, and full red lips. She invites me for a weekend.

Her father is a University of Chicago professor and her parents live in a dark apartment on Chicago's south side, furnished with old comfortable chairs and sofas. Immediately I feel at home. I spend hours talking to her mother and playing their piano, because at Downer (despite the Miss Erbe debacle) I miss a piano most of all.

This night we have dates with Gage and Jack. Gage drives, I'm in the back seat with Jack. Until now having to meet in public places has checked our hot romance. Now we're in the comparative privacy of a car.

I'm wearing a plain brown corduroy dress with a front zipper and a full skirt. To dress it up, I borrowed two amber clips from Phoebe's mother to anchor the v-neck open. I regret the clips the moment I slide into the back seat. It smells like a danger zone.

"Drink up." Jack finds my hand and shoves a flask into it. I hesitate, then toss burning liquid down my throat. I choke, then feel a glow flooding up and out from between my thighs. He presses his lips to my ear.

"Hi, Baby."

"Hi, Honey."

"Alone at last."

"Not *quite* alone."

"They don't count." He tilts back his head to drink from the flask again, a street light illuminating his sharp, bobbing Adam's apple. "You know what you told me this morning."

"No, what?" I've told him many things.

"You told me about the signal."

"Signal—"

"—Yeah. You said, swear to god now: 'If I wear a low-cut dress tonight that means we go all the way.'"

A chill like the east wind off Lake Michigan quenches my glow. I shiver.

"I never did!"

"Honey, you did. '*All the way*,' you said. You promised."

Am I going mad? *Did I say those words?* Never, never! Yet what if my mind's playing tricks. What if I really did agree to go all the way and am now conveniently "forgetting"? After all, I asked Phoebe for the pins to create that plunging neckline. But innocently, I tell myself—even aesthetically? Now I realize it's his word against mine.

Suddenly Jack Reed is sinister.

In a north Chicago suburb we pull up to a house so dark I think nobody's home, but when we ring, the front door opens. A streetlight shining through French doors is the only illumination. Shapes emerge, dissolve. I know they're real because occasionally I collide with a body. Whispers, bursts of laughter, reek of gin like wet pine needles.

I know that at last I'm really in danger, trapped by my irresistible urge to show off with boys, play the *femme fatale.*

Elsie never talks about sex, Emma raves about little else. Despite the thick red book by Dr. X hidden on Elsie's closet shelf, I know nothing about preventing pregnancy. Except, of course, by not going all the way.

Phoebe and Gage vanish. Jack pulls me to him. Again I realize what a superb dancer he is: that crouch, those liquid movements. We dance cheek to cheek to "I Can Dream, Can't I?" Jack humming the words in my ear:

> I'm aware my heart is a sad affair,
> There's much disillusion there,
> But I can dream, can't I?

Before I know he's danced me into a small room, kicked the door shut, backed me up against a bed. My knees buckle, I flop backward onto a pile of coats. He knows this house, I realize: he's danced other girls into this room. Fabric rips; his burning lips gobble me.

"Suck hoor!" Emma is shouting on the landing. "Spreading your legs for every dirty dog in town!"

I raise my fists, I beat at his head and shoulders, at the same time wrenching myself out from under him and sliding off the bed. Holding my ruined dress together with one hand, I crawl across the rug, find the door, and stumble out into a living room dense with cigarette smoke and heavy breathing. Somebody's put that song on again:

> I can see
> No matter how near you be
> You'll never belong to me—

"*Phoebe!*"

"Yo."

On the drive back to Phoebe's apartment Jack huddles against the far door glaring out the window, cigarette dangling from his lip, shoulder hunched against me. I know clearly now that I never said I'd go all the way. I know also that Emma saved me. This time.

CHAPTER TWENTY-FIVE

I know what Rob studied his junior year: *Macbeth, The Ballad and the Source,* Cicero, Dorothy Parker, *Hamlet, A Midsummer Night's Dream,* Sinclair Lewis, *The Rape of the Lock, The Mill on the Floss.* I knit him a black, white, and maroon ski sweater, one of my few sustained activities. It takes me until May to tie the last loop.

Grey, patient Miss Otto lugs me through Latin translations, I paint fashion designs under the northern skylights of Mrs. Tuteur's art room, I write a mystery story for Mrs. Van Wagenen in which the victim, stabbed at a Steinway grand, spells out the name of the murderer with his fingers on the keys.

The rest of my junior year is a blank.

One day in late March, as I come through the conservatory from my last class, Vera beckons me with a finger.

"Gentleman's waiting for you in the lounge."

"Gentleman" can not possibly describe Donald Allan. I debate rushing upstairs to put on lipstick (no make-up during school hours), instead hurry across the hall clutching my books to my chest. In the lounge a tall man in a black overcoat is standing at the window. He turns.

"Pickens!"

"Greetings. Your housemother tells me you have a free hour. I thought I might persuade you to take a walk."

"Well, gee—sure."

"Then get your coat."

He drives us to a park overlooking Lake Michigan where Lake Shore Drive swings up past the Water Plant from the lake. Except for two kids on swings, it's deserted. Patches of dirty snow stain the brown grass. Among the trees the air is cold, as if winter forgot to take it with her. Last year's oak leaves hang overhead like dead bats. I light a cigarette and shrug deeper into my coat, hiding the singed right sleeve. Pickens stoops to pick up a broken branch, twirls it between leather-gloved thumb and forefinger, flings it away.

"I like parks this time of year. They're empty."

"Yes." What he liked, I liked.

We walk in silence. He stops, presses down one end of a teeter-totter, fastidiously balances the board with his gloved palm, lets it go.

"I have to tell you something, Margo."

"Oh, yes?" Since I *know* what's he's going to say, he's going to say "I can't see you any more," I feel a spasm of pain.

He reaches for my icy hands and covers them with his gloves.

"I'm sad to say that your aunt and I have broken off our friendship."

I look up at him. I am five-feet six but he must be over six feet tall. A white scar I'd not noticed before gleams thinly on his right cheekbone. Not Leslie Howard, but George McCready, the suave villain of *Gilda*—that's who he reminds me of, with his fine, prematurely white hair, his fine tailored body, his white high-boned face.

But Pickens is a good man.

"Sorry," I say. "Oops, that sounds so trite." By now Pickens must know me for what I am, a raw high school junior.

Pickens turns his head away. "She was—is—a fine woman."

"Of course."

"With many fine—I may say, *noble*—qualities."

I stop and face him, I put my hand on his well-tailored coat sleeve.

"Too damn noble, Pickens."

I see a shadow slide down and off his face. His forehead smooths. He laughs harshly.

"What do you mean?"

Still burning with Marie's injustice, I tell him about last spring's toilet seat episode.

"That's *it*, you see." He pounds a fist into a palm. "To invent a crisis out of nothing."

"Though Marie *was* responsible for what went on in the new dorm."

"Yes, of course. But her jumping to conclusions, her accusations! As though you and your friend were criminals. It's not—" He stops short in the path, fastidiously turns over a chunk of snow with a polished toe. Leaf decay and dirt stain the underside.

"Normal?"

"I'd rather call it an over-developed sense of duty."

"Plus a terror of sex."

"My dear child!"

"I'm just guessing."

He laughs ruefully. "I do blame that terrible sense of responsibility of hers. Finally it *weighted* our friendship. I felt . . . oppressed."

"Blame my grandmother, Emma Merkel. She warped us all."

"Not you, darling, surely."

Darling? The path sways under my feet. It's the first time he's called me anything but "Margo."

"Especially me."

Our eyes meet. His are detached but inviting.

I know he wants me.

He gets me back to campus at five to five, pulling up to the curb and opening his door to get out. "No, please don't walk me to the front door!" For some reason I am horrified somebody might see me with him.

"I wonder." He gazes over the roofs of the Sem. "Would you care to have dinner sometime? Oh, I realize you're constantly 'booked up,' as they say. But perhaps some Friday?" He laughs self-consciously. "I'm quite bad at this. Consider it a duty to your Aunt's aging friend. Consider you're bringing me *au current*. I don't see my sister's teenagers nearly as often as I'd like."

No, Margo: no.

"Yes, I'd like to."

"This Friday, perhaps?"

"Fine."

"Pick you up at seven then. You *can* get out of this place, can't you?"

"This week I can."

This man I don't pin on my bulletin board. What I do is secretly draw hearts in all my school notebooks. In each center I ink in the initials "P.J."

Three Fridays in a row we eat at the same restaurant on Oakland Avenue. Kalt's is dark, with red-and-white checked table cloths and moody candles stuck in Chianti bottles. We seem to be getting along, but every so often he takes my hand, presses it between both of his and smiles as though someone's driving a knife into his heart.

One night leaving Kalt's we pause on the sidewalk to admire the night sky. Above the lights of Oakland Avenue a new moon hangs in the west. I drop his arm. "Silverkin," I whisper. "Lady's Slipper. Cradlekin."

Pickens raises an eyebrow. "Friend of yours?"

"Yes," I say, rubbing tears from my eyes.

This night when he pulls over to the curb in front of the Seminary he turns to me, rests his hand lightly on my shoulder.

"Could I interest you in coffee and a little music at my place?"

An hour and a half before check-in time. Margo, *no*.

"Gee, sure."

I'm the one who starts it; he who pulls back, trembling, white hair spilling over his forehead.

"My god, no, we can't do this. After all, I have *some* standards!"

I recoil. "*And I don't?*"

"I don't mean that, Margo darling. I mean I'm the adult here, I'm the responsible party."

"Oh, yes, that terrible sense of responsibility you admire so much."

He stands up, stuffing his shirt inelegantly into his pants.

"I'm taking you home."

"*Home!*"

"All right, back to the Sem. Come on, kiddo." His voice is unsteady. "Get your coat."

It's only lying in bed that night, staring out my window at a starless sky, that I realize how crazy I've been; how lucky that Marie's alienating sense of responsibility woke in Pickens Johnson.

After that it is never the same between us. Our walks in the park, oak buds swelling, children, mothers and dogs invading our private territory, become exercises in torment.

"I can't go on like this, darling, I really can't. I am not made of stone. I was insane to start this. You're a child."

I look up at the tree above our heads. Still those dead bats. Either oaks love their leaves or oak leaves love their trees. A sharp wind off the lake waters my eyes. I can feel my nose turning red.

"I'm seventeen next month."

"*A child.*"

I adore his anguish; it excites me. Nights in bed thinking of him I groan and knead my pillow, luxuriating in his pain.

I also pity him. He is a fine man.

One day he says: "There is a way, you know. A way you'd run no risk of getting pregnant."

Even Elsie's daughter has heard of condoms.

"You mean you'd wear a rubber?" I look longingly at the plum-dark lake. It's chopped by whitecaps but I'd like to be out there risking my life, anything but dueling with Pickens Johnson.

"Not that."

I light a Pall Mall, shielding my fag with cupped hand.

"I could teach you to enjoy it, you know."

"Pickens, I don't know what you're talking about."

"Come on. A precocious young woman like you?"

"I'm not!" I turn on him, furious. I think he's said "promiscuous."

"All right, but if you loved me, you'd help me."

I might have helped him if I had a clue. I don't.

Suddenly I feel terribly oppressed by this older man and his torment. Persecuted—*weighted down.* What has happened to my "rational adult"?

"I have to go."

He reaches automatically for his car keys.

"No, thanks." I'm walking backward, away from him, putting the greening grass between us step by step as fast as I can. I see now that we are a promise I must break. "Good bye. Call me." I can't smile, instead I wave hopelessly and run. When I look over my shoulder, he's standing among the oaks, hands thrust in pockets, his head bowed.

"Gotta tell you something," says Phoebe. We're walking back up Downer Avenue, fatter by two triple-dip hot fudge pecan sundaes topped with whipped cream and a cherry.

"What?" I swing my purse extravagantly against my leg. New leaves are uncurling above my head. I feel full and suave and contented.

"I don't want to room with you next year."

My purse falls to the sidewalk.

"What?" I am too stunned to say anything more. My rooming with Phoebe senior year is a done deal. We're going to have a blast.

I bend to pick up the purse. "*Why* ?" I finally croak.

"I'm rooming with Vivian Rice. We've got the big end room, Viv and J.Z.'s old double. It's settled."

"But *why*?"

"Because of how you acted in Chicago."

Chicago: Phoebe's parents home. I'm bewildered. "How did I act?"

She flings her black hair forward, a thick black curtain across her face, tosses it back. "Jesus Christ, half the time you sat there *talking to my mother*. I freaked out. And you were always playing our piano. *Classical* music, Chrissake!"

O god: this is all over again my best friend Mary Jane Hovden suddenly finding a new girl in third grade to walk to school with. Deserting me, forcing me to walk with Wayne Gnirk, short with red ears, famous for having hiccups five days in a row, ahead of us sauntering Mary Jane and Gina Olsen in tiny loafers and twin sets—gossiping, giggling, swinging hands.

I must defend myself, I must fight.

"Sure, I felt comfortable with your parents, why not? All my life I've lived with adults, I'm an only child. I dig the Ink Spots and Frankie Lane more than you do! I neck in back seats just like you. I smoke, I drink. You don't dare dump me!" Instead I mumble: "What's wrong with Beethoven and Mozart?"

"If you have to *ask*!"

We walk in silence until she spots Vivian and Jan Monroe half a block ahead.

"This is Pitsville." She breaks into a trot. "So long."

Three days later, on my way to chapel, I find a letter in my box.

Please see me in my office after classes today at four.
Nar Warren Taylor.

Déja vu.

This time, though, I am terrified.

None of my classes have been going particularly well. In French Mlle Witmer calls on me to conjugate the verb *tenir;* I blank, stumble, fall. "Epouvantable!" she hisses, sooty mustache bunching under her nose. "E-p-o-u-v-a-n-t-a-b-l-e," she chalks on the blackboard. She's a tiny woman, everything she writes on the blackboard is below eye-level, you have to stand up from your desk to see it. "Dégoutante!"

When finally I drag myself to Nar Warren Taylor's office I'm already feverish. "Peaches" Rhone, her secretary, beams at me, but since Mrs. Rhone gets her nickname because in her world everything's always peachy, I take no comfort.

Miss Taylor wears the moss-green suit and pearl earrings. She has knotted a silk paisley scarf about her throat. Barricaded behind her desk—safe, unimpregnable—she again dimples at me without smiling. I slip into the chair opposite.

"Ah suppose you know why ah've asked to see you today."

I don't and I do.

"I regret having to say this, Margo, but I can't approve the renewal of your scholarship for next year."

For three and a half semesters, I've been daring this to happen—been shouting defiance from the rooftops, shoving rebellion down authority's throat. Nevertheless I am outraged.

"I don't understand!"

"I have here the J-Board report as well as your grades going into finals. As it stands, your grade point is a disappointing 2.4. You do realize that's not nearly good enough."

Suddenly I'm back in third grade, Superintendent of Schools visiting, shooting up my hand because he's asked somebody to spell *angel*. "Margo," says Mrs. Kersten confidently. "Angel," I say: "a-n-g-l-e."

I hate Nar Warren Taylor, I loved Mrs. Kirsten. The shame is the same.

"But if I really buckle down for finals—"

Her eyes slide over me like snakes.

"As for demerits, fifteen is the maximum any Downer student can accumulate without being suspended. *Do you have any idea how many demerits you have on your record?*"

Suddenly I really hate her. And I have one talent she doesn't.

"But, Miz Taylah, ah've been workin' off them demerits aftah schoo-al in study ha-awl."

She stiffens in outrage and I know that Emma has possessed my tongue. I've always been a good mimic but this was not the time to practice my gift. Or maybe, knowing I'm past saving, I did it deliberately?

Her cheeks dimple deep as bullet holes.

"You have earned thirty-five demerits this school year. I am given to understand, Margo, that no student in the history of Milwaukee Downer Seminary has ever compiled such a disgraceful record."

I turn look down, I can take this. But I can't. Tears flood my cheeks, stream into my mouth down my chin into my neck. I can't stop them.

She opens a drawer, nudges a box of Kleenex across her desk to me with her knuckles.

I reach blindly for the box, but the tears won't stop: I choke and sob, I wail and shudder. She leans back, waits me out with unthawed eyes.

"Does—does my aunt know?" I gasp, groping for more tissues. Oh, God: not only stealing her boy friend but wasting her hopes and money.

"Miz Merkel has been informed, as has Miz Holmes. Apart from the four of us, the matter is confidential. If you wish to keep it so."

Unable to speak, I nod yes.

She shoots a cuff and glances at the man's watch on her left wrist.

"That will be all."

I stumble out of her office, swiping snot on my sweater sleeve, run blindly to the first exit and head for the tennis court. In ten minutes the dorm bell will ring for five-fifteen study.

It's a cruel day in late April, wind off the lake. The tennis court is deserted, so is the hockey field. A flag snaps angrily, chain clanking against its pole. A burst of rain freckles the green tennis asphalt. I walk blindly toward the link fence. Something dark is stuck in its web. I move close. It's a blackbird, one broken red wing stiffly angled. They're the first to venture north in spring.

I close my hand over the bird and ease it out, I nurse it in my hand. It is cold. *"Stupid bird, what are you doing, so far from your marsh? You could have flown higher."*

I shove the bird under a leaf, it doesn't care now. I count on my fingers the now-empty rituals I must endure before end of term. Upper School Fun Day, the Talent Show, Junior-Senior prom, Field Day, Father-Daughter Sports Day Banquet, Final Honors Assembly, Baccalaureate and Commencement practice. Not to mention parties, photographs, shopping for gifts, final exams, and Baccalaureate and Commencement themselves.

All Downer seniors have juniors as flower girls. My cool senior is Nini Ramsey, pale green eyes, freckles, a sense of humor dry as our Latin teacher's chalk. For Commencement, I have a new pale lavender formal with a floating skirt and whispers of organdy about the shoulders. To the solemnities of "Pomp and Circumstance," I will be walking behind Nini up the aisle of the Congregational Church on Kenwood Boulevard carrying flowers which I will present to her after Nar Warren hands her her diploma. "I know the dress is expensive, Marie," I'd pleaded, again at Emma Lange's, "but it's totally economical because I can wear it next year for Senior Prom *and* graduation."

How Nini will despise me. How everyone will despise me. And through it all I will smile and laugh and pretend I'm having an absolute panic.

"Your aunt wants you to call her," says Vera. She cocks an eyebrow, perhaps because my face is swollen with tears, perhaps because at last I'm punctual for study, now that it doesn't matter. Vera and Marie seem to be thick.

I cannot call Marie. I lug my feet upstairs, flop onto my bed, pull my pillow over my head. I'm cried out, I just want to sleep.

That June I walk into chapel for the last time. After announcements and valedictions, we rise to sing a hymn. The senior class has chosen "Jerusalem":

> Bring me my bow of burning gold
> Bring me my arrows of desire.
> Bring me my spear, oh clouds unfold,
> Bring me my chariot of fire.
> I will not shrink from daily strife,
> Nor let the sword sleep in my hand
> Till I have built Jerusalem
> In every green and pleasant land.

Far more than any other ritual of Milwaukee Downer Seminary, the singing of William Blake's hymn at morning chapel has entered my soul.

I know now that I've been offered them all—golden bow, arrows of desire, spear, chariot of fire—and that I've thrown them all recklessly away. It's as though from the moment of my arrival at Milwaukee Downer Seminary I have done everything possible to sabotage my chances here. So I can go back to Emma.

CHAPTER TWENTY-SIX

Rob's letter of May 28, 1950 throws a life preserver to a drowning swimmer:

Thank you so much for your junior photo. It's beautiful. I've decided to relax my anti-vice crusade. You may smoke your precious Pall Malls to your heart's content.

You are hereby officially invited to the lake as soon as Downer's out. My mother has just written yours. Bring a tennis racket. There are also stables: bring your boots and riding crop and teach me to ride. My father says he's very sorry he can't pick you up in Milwaukee—he goes back to Des Moines the day after he delivers us to Delavan. Fortunately there are buses. From Delavan take a cab to our cottage. Everyone knows where it is.

I cannot wait till June. You *must* come.

At Delavan I automatically play the adventuress. My expulsion from Downer only seems to add to my appeal, as does Donald's tracking me to the lake and pursuing us wherever we go. Yes, Rob lectures me, but he also lights my Pall Malls, hangs on my tales, shows me off to his friends, and is jealous enough to strip three ID bracelets off my wrist and hurl them into the lake. We have a panic, yet beneath high spirits I'm hollow with dread. From the beginning I've tried to tell Rob about Emma; he's always cut me off with an impatient "Just leave." I've always felt helpless to explain why we can't. Anyway, does he really want to know? Rob is the friend of Margo-pretend. He seems so dazzled by my line I can't imagine revealing my true self to him.

Impossible anyway, because I still don't know who that true self is.

Two weeks of dry heat, and I can see Delavan Lake shrinking, piers stretching farther into the lake. Every evening, though, as the sun slips behind the latest big lakeshore house, we gather on the pier to slap mosquitos, wait for the moon, and play "Rhythm." "One," shouts Rob, clapping hands twice, knees twice: "One-Five!" "Five" claps his hands, knees, shouts "Five-Seven."

"Seven" misses her cue because she's going over her options. They are damn few.

Marry Pickens? It's one thing marrying James Mason in my dreams, quite another marrying an actual forty-something man. Besides, he hasn't asked me. I sense he's ashamed of his passion and blames me for it. I felt it that bad day at the park. His impatient shrug, the hurting grip of his hand on my arm.

Jack hates St. John's. Yes, we talk about running away to get married, but Jack? I've hardly ever seen him in daylight: we haunt bars, restaurants, dance floors, backs of cars, a blacked-out house in a Chicago suburb. I don't really know him and I can't think of an interest of mine that he shares.

With fanatic Mr. Allan's blessing, Donald would marry me tomorrow. I can not marry Donald.

If I could only get a job and make enough money, Elsie and I could have our own apartment. But at seventeen I have no skills, no practical training.

I grab Rob's hands and taunt him about my lost ID bracelets until he shoves me shrieking into the lake.

The Faulkners drive me to Milwaukee, but drop me on an unfamiliar street on the South Side because Mrs. Faulkner is fussing about being late for lunch with relatives.

"*Sure* you don't mind, dear?"

"This is fine. Thanks again for a wonderful time."

But I mind terribly. When I cab to the Milwaukee Road station I find I don't have enough money for the train, so I lug my heavy suitcase to the bus depot. The hot, lonely ride goes on forever. What's the reverse of Good Queen Bess's triumphal "progresses" through her green and pleasant land? The return of the Prodigal, I suppose: the child of thriftlessness and waste. Unlike the Prodigal Son, however, no fatted calf will be slain for me, no wineskins tapped, no father's embrace.

With no money for a cab, I trust my suitcase to a sleepy attendant behind the counter, and begin the long trek up Washington Street. It is a warm, still June night. Raucous laughter spills from the open door of the tavern on the corner of Sixth. On the sidewalks of slum houses near the tracks, dirty-faced kids shriek and run barefoot hours past their bedtimes. Light glows behind the windows of the Fair Deal Grocery, but I see that Mr. Schumacher is just closing up. If I had a dime I'd buy an Eskimo

Pie just to hear him bang the cash register and shout, "Hallelujah, I'm a bum."

Past the tracks East Hill begins to climb. Houses are better here, porches more spacious, front lawns bigger, blacker squares. In an open window a stout woman sits at an upright playing "The Green Cathedral" and shaking her head impatiently at every wrong note. A few houses later shrilling crickets take over the night. A toad hops across the walk, I recoil. O god, venturing at twilight as a child across our cement patio strewn with early windfalls, one apple lurching under my foot, standing frozen, not daring to step forward or back.

Nobody's yet built on the corner lot of Tenth and Washington. The next house is the Petersens, or used to be, with the mammoth soft maple that remains Emma's personal anti-Christ. Its winged seeds choke her gutters, carpet her driveway and lawn. Year after year she makes threatening phone calls.

Next is 1016, the shabbiest house on the block.

I can hear Emma's chair rockers groaning on the dark front porch. She probably holds a saucepan in her lap, ready to throw coffee grounds on her geraniums. She loves flowers; if she hated weeds the way she hates that soft maple, she'd be a great gardener.

I want to walk on by, up the hill, past Aunt Hattie's and Helen's and my apple orchard. I want to duck under the barbed wire fence, run down the field, leap the stream and vanish into the heart of Pavy's Woods never to come back. Instead, I set my foot on the bottom porch step.

Emma's hand flies to her heart. Sarah Bernhardt couldn't have done the astonishment bit better.

"Land o' Light, you gave me a fright! Thought I was going to be murdered. What are *you* doing here this time of night!"

"I'm home from school."

She leans forward to toss the last of the coffee grounds toward a pot. She chuckles.

"I remember now, Marie said you'd be coming. Didn't make it in Milwaukee, did you? Just like your mother at Carroll. She went crazy, you know, bet you did too. Johnny'll be crawling back himself one of these days, mark my words. Thinks he's Mr. High and Mighty, thinks he can run with the big dogs. Marie too, got her head in the clouds, going to be Dean of that school. Don't worry, you'll all be back. Scraping on your bellies like dogs for a bone."

That summer of 1950 I am restless, unsettled, and terrified about re-entering Wausau High as a senior. Gone two years, I don't have any friends I feel I can call before school begins. Neither Winkelman's nor Penney's is hiring. John the Radio Announcer has vanished from Elsie's life. I have date or two. After one of them I get home about eleven, try the door. Locked. Side door: locked. Back door: locked. I'm so furious I run round the house banging and shouting "Open up!" A sudden light in a neighboring window halts me. I slump into a dank patio chair, pull out a Pall Mall, and start swatting mosquitos.

After midnight a car pulls into the drive, a door opens and shuts. I see a firefly glow brighten and dim. Home from a date, Elsie emerges from the dark, stealing a last smoke outdoors.

"Margo! What are you doing here!"

"Emma's locked the house. Let's yell and throw stones."

"Heavens, no! Think of the neighbors."

"What's *your* plan?"

"Let's walk downtown. Maybe there's a place open we can get a cup of coffee."

"Do you have any money?"

"Thirty cents."

"I've got a quarter."

The Third Street diner is lit so brightly we flinch as we walk in. We choose a booth, order coffee, look around. Who *are* these people? Nobody I've seen on the streets in daylight. Probably they're thinking the same about us. In thirty minutes our money runs out. A tired waitress slaps down the bill. "I'm gonna close." We retreat up the hill, huddle together on the bench under the Duchess apple tree, icy dew soaking our shoes, arms wrapped around each other to keep warm.

"Elsie, if we don't get out of here together, I'm getting out by myself."

She begins to sob.

Doesn't she realize I don't have a cent to go anywhere?

That August I walk in on the fight so I don't know how it began. The combatants are poised like toy soldiers on the staircase. Emma is sixty-five, my mother thirty-eight. Despite her age and 200 pounds, Emma has the advantage.

This time I don't run for the broom, I watch. Emma charges down the stairs, Elsie dodges and runs back up, Emma rampages after her. Emma and Elsie lock in struggle at the top.

"Bitch! Traitor! Sneaking my granddaughter away! For what? To rot in the streets like a Pollack, to be a hoor like you? Not a penny to your name and she'll spend it. You'll both end in the gutter, you and your slut—"

Elsie finds voice:

"Mother, I can't stand this any more, I can't take this any more, none of us can take it any more. We're leaving you, we're never coming back."

"Know why Edgar left you? He *despised* you—"

I've had enough. Feeling strangely incurious, I walk downtown and find a seat in the Grand in time to see Harry Lime thrust his fingers though a Viennese sewer lid, flex them helplessly, and disappear.

Two weeks later Elsie has rented an apartment. We don't have much to take away from Emma's house. Our clothes and Elsie's boxes of costume jewelry, my Underwood typewriter that survived smashing the storm window, a box or two of diaries, manicure sets, stationery, photograph albums, cosmetics. In my closet I go through the contents of my big hump-backed trunk, but the enchantments of my childhood have withered like last year's leaves and I let the heavy lid drop. Elsie is charging furniture around town at Merman's and Radant's. A corner desk and matching bookcases, end tables, a coffee table in the blond oak that's all the rage, a couch in fashionable chartreuse are going to be delivered to the apartment today. All that remains is to make it with our boxes out of Emma's house and into the ordered taxi.

"One last time!" says Elsie. She lifts her chin, squares her plump shoulders. "We'll never have to do this again, Honey."

"We may not *live* to do it again."

The house is quiet in a menacing way. Nothing, not even the squawk of Emma's radio.

We tiptoe down the stairs, pause on the landing. Emma's Windsor chair in front of the TV is empty.

"Where is she?"

"Must be in the kitchen."

"Let's not analyze further."

Twenty feet lie between us and the front door.

"Go!" I urge her forward.

Unbelievably, Elsie lingers at the door, hand on the knob.

"Bye, Mother," she calls. "We'll call as soon as we get a phone."

"Do you *want* a scene? *Go!*" I push her out of the house. The cab's at the curb.

So goodbye, Emma.

As though one can say goodbye to the tempest that bent the young branch.

CHAPTER TWENTY-SEVEN

So my story ends, or almost. In 1950 Elsie and I did escape and now have our own apartment. Elsie blossoms. She makes artistic and liberal friends, entertains, expands her society editor job to include covering cultural events. She buys new hats and shoes, eventually is named Wausau's Woman of the Year.

Yes, she calls Emma regularly and we visit 1016 Washington Street from time to time. But we have been liberated.

For years I thought our freedom was the result of Emma's and Elsie's fight on the stairs. I know now it was Marie. Marie had given Elsie enough money to find our own apartment and move out. I often think of what I owe her. The Underwood typewriter, the Parker pen, the dictionary. Milwaukee Downer when it became crucial I leave Emma's house. Flights to Des Moines, trips to Delavan, party gowns, riding lessons, a train to Peoria. In my future: the tuition to finish my BA at the University of Wisconsin-Madison. What have I ever given her?

Before my senior year begins, popular Mary Boileau invites me to a slumber party at her house, an invitation important enough to baptize me a member of Wausau High's in-group. I care about being in (after being out all my life); but it's also important to me to be with girls I've always liked: Bette Irwin, Claire Hennig, Jane Holman, Mary herself. As for the "in" senior boys, they seem very young.

All my life I've continued to search for answers to my great puzzles. (I now know why I feel the wind when the sun goes under a cloud—though, as the poet Lorine Niedecker says, I do not yet know the law of the oak leaf.) My childhood is a wound that never healed. If I dig deep, cauterize this wound with a fiery brand, can I, finally, heal?

What really, for instance, went wrong with my parents' marriage?

I get an unexpected answer in 2001 when Elsie is eighty-nine. I'm driving her around Lake Mills, Wisconsin, on errands. Lake Mills is a small city between Madison and Milwaukee where we both (co-incidentally) live—also Johnny who, indeed, has been forced to sell his sailboat, give up his Annapolis apartment, and "crawl,"(as Emma would rave) back to Wisconsin where he promptly moved in with his sister. He bosses Elsie unbearably; she's as little able to stand up to him as she was to Emma.

In the midst of errands Elsie says, "Let's go to Bouslough's and arrange for Johnny's funeral."

I laugh. Johnny is healthy, and besides has already taken care of his own funeral arrangements. Oh, the resentments seething hot under the crust of Fandamily. But Elsie's frankness surprises her, I think, and releases other truths.

"Your father, Edgar, thought he was really something. Once he insisted I go up in a plane with him, though I didn't want to at all. Then who got violently sick while I was cool as a cucumber?" She gazes out the car window, waves to objects: "Hello, tree! Hello, lake! Hello, clouds." She has a passion for clouds. "They're changing and beautiful and don't cost a cent." Then she says, quite casually: "I never wanted to get married, all I ever wanted was to be an actress. *Never did I want to be a wife.*"

And there it is, at last. The Depression, Emma hating the marriage, 1016 too crowded for Edgar to move in, Edgar leaving

Wausau to find work, Edgar sending for us from Chicago—all that's been evasion and lies. Elsie didn't want to be married, to any man. Solved, at last.

Then, in 2012, I reconnect with Pat Ann, that favorite cousin who assured me olives were an acquired taste.

"I remember my mom, Hattie, saying, 'If it wasn't for Emma, Elsie and Edgar would still be married. Emma could poison anybody's mind against a person she hated.' Your grandmother broke up your parents' marriage, Margo. She wove a spell that cast Edgar McCullough and his whole family as devils incarnate. Your mother couldn't fight that spell. She gave in; she let your father go."

I married and give birth to my first child, Mark John, on October 7, 1955. Less than three weeks later, Marie called. Grandfather had not come down at seven a.m. to collect his hot water and carry it upstairs to the bathroom where he shaved with a straight razor in the cloudy bathroom mirror. Eventually Emma found him in bed; he had died in his sleep. Putting down the phone, I realize that Grandfather will never see his only great-grandson. As for his funeral, I beg off: trying to nurse, can't leave Mark with a sitter, long haul to Wausau with a new baby.

But it wasn't the new baby. Though I'd escaped her house five years ago, I still hadn't forgiven this mild, blue-eyed gentleman for not saving me from Emma. I don't know whether he ever forgave *me* for not understanding him before he died.

Three years later, I have one last confrontation with Emma Merkel. Marie has semi-retired to Wausau as part-time counselor at the local college and full-time martyr at home. One weekend, however, there's a conference she wants to attend. As usual Johnny's not around, I don't know where Elsie is, but in any case she won't be any good: all her life she's refused woman's work like cooking, sewing, cleaning and nursing, so that no one expects her to do it. Clever Elsie. Marie asks me to come for the weekend.

"Mother will love seeing Mark."

No.

I haven't set foot in 1016 Washington Street in years, and am still in shock about Elsie giving away the entire contents of my childhood trunk to itinerant neighbors. Just the thought of returning so agitates me that I light my new brand, Winstons. That night I also dream again the dream. The front sidewalk scalds my bare legs as I play jacks. Hours pass, the sun drops behind trees. Gradually I become aware that something behind my back has changed.—the house, it shimmers evil. I scramble up, I'll run to the neighbors. But, one by one, the neighbors' lights wink out.

I've taught myself to wake from this dream before the lights go out. And I'm married and grown-up. And I owe Marie debts I can never repay. I say yes.

Emma is sitting as close to the kitchen table as her stomach permits, listening to polkas on the radio. Three-year-old Mark runs to her. Her crutch balances against the table. I don't look at her bare purple legs.

"Watch Grandma's legs!" she warns, then kisses him. "Is you hungry?" She said that to me when I was little, I loved to hear her say it. "I bet you is!" Fortunately she doesn't bake anymore and Mark gets a Lorna Doone.

We're settling in upstairs when I hear a slammed door, a crutch stumping to the bottom of the stairs.

"Fucking hoor! Sneaking bitch—"

Mark's blue eyes grow round.

Quite calmly I throw our things back into the suitcase, take Mark's hand, lead him downstairs and out the side door, stow him in the back seat of the car. "It's all right, Mark love. Stay here and play with Bear. Back in a minute."

I find her crouched behind her Windsor chair. Her crutch lies on the floor. She glares at me like a wild animal.

"*God damn you*," I say. "You've done your filthy best to ruin everybody's life—your husband's, sisters', John's, Elsie's, Marie's. And mine. But I'm not afraid of you. You have a choice. You can shut your mouth and behave like a human being while I'm here or you can watch me drive away. I have a car. And I'm not Marie. And I don't give a god damn whether you live or die. You can rot in hell."

She's panting, foam flecks her lips.

"All right," I say, "I'm going."

I have the car in reverse when a movement at the kitchen window makes me look up. She's rapping with her knuckles at the pane, the rap from childhood. It was the way she summoned me from sledding or playing or reading under the green canopy. She never stepped outside to call, she rapped.

The sun's going down. I think of my nightmare of the house changing to evil behind my back. Maybe she's having it now.

Let her.

POSTLUDE

One day in 1997 I receive a note signed "Joan McCullough Lyntz." My first cousin has seen my name in a newspaper, can we meet for lunch? Joan turns out to be the daughter of my father's oldest brother, Wesley McCullough.

"You know, Joan, I've tried contacting my father from time to time, but never got an answer. Do you have any idea where he lives?"

"Here's his address and phone number."

In December I fly to Santa Barbara, rent a car, and drive north along Highway 1 to Paso Robles. Edgar has reserved a room for me at the historic Paso Robles Inn. He calls for me. For years I've had a photograph of him in my study. Friends always exclaim, "Who's the movie star!" I recognize him immediately.

At eighty-six he is still strikingly handsome: over six feet tall, slender, broad-shouldered. White hair falling in natural waves (as mine does), salt and pepper eyebrows thickly male, complexion ruddy. His hands are long; once artistic, I guess, now distorted by arthritis. He wears an immaculate grey pin-striped suit, a blue and white-striped shirt, a silvery blue tie. His feet in highly-polished cordovan tassel loafers are elegantly narrow.

We shake hands formally. If we're nervous or apprehensive neither of us shows it. Thanks to Emma (is this a good thing?) I am protected from my emotions by a carapace that must be three-feet thick. I never cried, all those years of living with her.

In my opera-loving family, I always yearned for what I called "the Voice of the Father." My aural life was woven from the timbres of Grandfather's tenor, Marie's alto, Mother's soprano, Johnny's charming Cary Grant, Emma's dramatic and terrifying coloratura. What I missed, viscerally, was the dark bass of singers like Chaliapin, Boris Christoff, Caesar Siepi, Fischer-Diskau, Bryn Terfel. I wait tensely, therefore, for Edgar McCullough's voice.

"How was your flight? Did you have any trouble finding Paso Robles?"

It is neither high nor low, it rises and falls: a pleasing, versatile baritone. Like Elsie, he speaks impeccable English.

He is not my "Voice of the Father."

He escorts me to a sports vehicle he calls a "Jimmy." At the wheel, he explains that he lives with Marilyn McWilliams, "whose family owns half of Paso Robles. We've been together thirty years. We're not married, I pay her rent."

Marilyn, dark, plump and younger than Edgar I'd guess by twenty years, welcomes me warmly to a contemporary house set into a hill.

"We're going to have a drink," Edgar explains, "then go to the Paso Robles Inn for dinner.

When I see a Baldwin organ against a wall, I turn to him, radiant.

"You play! So do I."

"Not so much any more. I've let the thing get badly out of tune."

"Please play something for me. I still have your music."

"Music?"

"You left three signed pieces of sheet music in the piano bench at 1016 Washington." I hate saying this, I'll sound needy, but I do: "I've treasured them."

He only gestures dismissively at the organ. "Too out of tune, believe me. It's been a long, long time."

I feel a second jolt when he offers me champagne—my favorite drink. From the moment we shook hands, he has felt eerily familiar to me. I watch him now from across the room. He seems detached and alone, yet is frequently amused. He leans forward when he laughs, hands on his knees; bursts into dramatizations, chiefly of himself: "*What* am I thinking!" "*Where* did I put those keys!" I sense vitality, I sense volatility. I sense he is outgoing, but deeply reserved.

Marilyn seems eager to tell me about him.

"Edgar and I live together, but he's the most independent guy I've ever known! Does his own laundry, makes his own coffee and breakfast before I'm out of bed. Very private: won't let me into his bedroom or study."

"Now, Marilyn," he says irritably, "we don't have to talk about that."

But Marilyn laughs, prods him.

"Bring out your photograph albums for Margo. Margo wants to know about things, she has a right to know." I've brought a photo album too. We bend heads over pictures. I draw my breath at a portrait of a beautiful woman with black hair parted in the middle, beautiful bones, wide-set dark eyes.

"Edgar's second wife, Marie," says Marilyn, seemingly without envy. 'What a gorgeous couple they made."

Indeed: Marie rivals Hedy Lamar. Poor Elsie.

Edgar flips the page, says shortly: "She died on the operating table in 1963 of brain cancer."

"I'm terribly sorry." I am. "Who are these?"

"Your brother Scott and your sister Sharon."

I have half-siblings! I never imagined the possibility, though how inevitable.

"Where do they live?"

"Sharon works for Universal Pictures in Los Angeles. Scott"—he shakes his head—"who knows? Ran away from home at sixteen on his motorcycle. Moved in with an older woman. Not just any older woman: *Black*."

We talk no further about Scott. I show him photos taken at our lake house on Little Bearskin in Wisconsin's north woods. "Gorgeous scenery, what a beautiful collie!"

He says nothing about the center of the photograph, my beautiful daughter Claire. He says nothing about photographs of my handsome son Marc. *Why?* Neither does he ask, and I don't offer to tell him, about my life. That after two misjudged marriages, I'm happily married at last. That my two grown children, Marc and Claire, are both married and living close in Sun Prairie and Madison. That I took early retirement from the English and Women's Studies Departments at the University of Wisconsin-Whitewater in 1991, that I'm a writer with ten published books.

Marilyn tops my glass with champagne. "Your father has a very high I.Q., Margo. Did you know he graduated from school at sixteen, then went to the County Normal where he majored in English? He taught one year in a country school, lived with his family during the week."

My father taught English? I have a PhD in English literature, and all these years so sure I had nothing in common with this man.

I don't remember who brings up Elsie. Probably Marilyn.

He leans back, cocking the ankle of one long leg over a knee. His face is neutral.

"I never had any quarrel with your mother."

He will say this many times during my stay.

"But you did divorce. Why?"

"I was working in an office. One morning your mother sent a message from the lawyers: 'Yes or no? Divorce or not?' My clerk didn't give it to me until late afternoon, she'd wanted my answer right away. I'm a person who never looks back, I make a decision and stick to it. A fatalist. I said, 'Well, that's that, too late to do anything about it, that's the way it was meant to be.'"

Not satisfactory. He was working in an office, she sent him a note. Had they already separated? Was the divorce only her idea? This fits with her, "I only wanted to be an actress." I look at him, pleading.

"Was it Emma Merkel?"

He looks at Marilyn, looks away, crosses his arms over his chest.

Oh, god, there's so much I want to know, if only I could talk to you alone! I can't, with Marilyn here, kind though she is. *And you know that. That's why she's here.*

He does tell me this: He moved to Chicago in 1937, got a job as a floor manager for Marshall Field's; met Marie, a buyer for the silverware and china department; married her. Therefore, when he met up with Elsie in Chicago in 1943, he had a second wife.

"You were in the Air Force. You were a pilot." I'd always imaged him flying dangerous missions over Berlin or Tokyo. In grade school I drew bombers and fighter planes in my lose-leaf notebook, pretending my father was at the controls.

"Never a pilot. I spent the war very comfortably, thank you, at an air base in California, near Paso Robles. That's when I fell in love with this countryside."

That evening at the Inn we eat formally, sitting far apart in a large round booth. I realize that nothing will be revealed here over the white-tablecloth and the knot of artificial flowers in the vase. He has planned this, far in advance. He orders steak, Marilyn chicken, me shrimp—as though this matters. Our talk is stilted, neutral, and far too much about what we're eating. Mentally, though, I file away every word he says.

That night I make myself a cup of tea from the courtesy tray, scrunch pillows behind my back, and reflect upon the day. Edgar and I have been alone for exactly the twenty minutes it took to drive from the Inn to Marilyn's house. I've already been informed of tomorrow's plans: Hearst Castle and other points of interest, with Marilyn; eat at a restaurant on the Coast that he loves, with Marilyn; then he'll drive me back to the Inn, with Marilyn, to collect my car. I'll be in Santa Barbara by early evening.

I've come so far, after so many many years. It can't end this way.

It *will* end this way, Margo. What did you expect from a two-day meeting with a father you haven't seen in sixty-one years?

I screw the cap off one of those mini bottles in the courtesy fridge. What did I learn today about my father?

He's interested in money, this is key. No one in our family knows beans about money, even Marie, though she finally managed to pay off the 1016 Washington mortgage before she died.

Edgar loves to dance. Deep-sea fishes. "I used to read constantly." Watches PBS. *Hates* Barbra Streisand—another taste in common, though *hate* is a word I reserve for a choice few.

Drinks Margaritas.

Gambles, "very cautiously. Black jack at Vegas. When dealers used two decks I could memorize every card, gave it up when they began using three."

Disgusted with way football's played today.

Energy.

Racist: anti Hispanic, anti Black.

Old-fashioned manners. High spirits, quick temper, love of a good story, sentimental in a canny way. Strict parent, I would guess.

He and M. play poker for pennies every night. (*Frisson*: I love poker.) He & M talk over each other constantly. She interrupts him, he interrupts her: "I've been darn good to you."

I turn out the light.

Next morning a surprise tour as he drives Marilyn and me around the acres of a chicken ranch he still owns. Never have I associated my father with chickens.

"Raised nine million, owned fourteen big ranches from Salinas to south of Paso Robles. Sold chickens to Swift, then sold one of the ranches to Buster Keaton, another to Tim Holt, gradually got out of the chicken business and went into real estate, drove around in a big red Lincoln continental. I've worked hard and I'm tight with money, believe me. (I believe him: the bicycle.) Marilyn and I keep our money entirely separate. Her brother gypped her out of seven million, but she's still damn well-off."

Gradually I understand that Edgar did not clean chicken pens for a living. He was an entrepreneur. Still . . . . chickens? Yet how Elsie and I could have used some good old-fashioned egg money.

By noon the time left to us together is so brief I've already kissed it goodbye. Above all I want to touch him, I want him to touch me. We climb into the Jimmy, drive west to the Hearst palace, Marilyn kindly allowing me to sit in front. Edgar is silent, Marilyn chatty, reaching forward to turn my head to look things of interest. (Hands off, please.) I dislike the landscape: bleached and dry, so unlike green Wisconsin. Edgar leads Marilyn and me on a tour I know he's suffered many times. Useless, if it's to impress me. Hearst Castle is an impersonal tomb.

Back in the car: "How's Johnny?" he asks unexpectedly. "Still alive?" His voice resonates, I vibrate to its vitality.

"Doing well for eighty-seven."

He shakes his head. "*Never one of the guys, Johnny, you know?* Different."

He's telling me my uncle was gay?

"A great man for the ladies," I say defensively.

He whips around a Dodge van. "See that? Guy's wearing a hat. Ever noticed bad drivers always wear hats? But Johnny never married."

"True."

But I'm not about to explore my uncle with an unknown father. The Johnny I know flirts with women. No, he never married. How could he, when Emma ruined him for women even while he sought them? Years later, I will learn that Aunt Hattie too thought Johnny was homosexual. I don't know, and I don't know how to answer Edgar, whose questions I don't like. Perhaps he lumps gays with his despised Blacks and Hispanics. For me Johnny was a man. He wore suits, drove cars, shaved, bossed people around, sent women flowers, led when we did the rhumba.

"Anyway," says Edgar, shooting a glance at me at last. His eyes are hazel, like Emma's. I place great importance on eyes. "I want you to know something, I'm serious now, so remember what I'm telling you. Any brains you've got you get from your mother and her family. I mean that."

We eat a late lunch at his favorite restaurant on the coast, a sea-food shack built into a cliff just off the highway, with views of flat, rhythmic surf.

Marilyn leans forward over her crab salad. "I don't care, sweetheart, I'm telling Margo about the arrowheads."

"We don't have to talk about that." My father's voice contains a warning.

"No, really." She locks my left wrist with her hand. "Edgar took me to this resort in New Mexico, all day we hunted for arrowheads, no luck. Next morning he says, let's try again. So we go over the same ground and my god, arrowheads everywhere! 'And you wanted to give up without trying,' he says.

"Well, we're driving home, he's all red in the face, bent over the wheel snorting with laughter. Finally he says, 'I got to tell you, Marilyn, I can't drive another mile, I sneaked out early this morning, I went and planted those arrowheads for you.'

"First I'm speechless because I've been cradling the damn things like a baby two hundred miles on my lap, planning how I'm going to get a stunning necklace made and buy a display case lined with black velvet for the rest. *And he planted them?* Let me tell you: I exploded. I rolled down my window and threw out every goddam arrowhead. And did I chew out Edgar!"

I look at him, gauging his mood. His head is turned away from me; he says stiffly:

"We don't have to talk about that, Marilyn."

They say fruit doesn't fall far from the tree. This very fall— because every time we tramp our acres at the north end of Rock Lake in Lake Mills, Wisconsin, my husband says, "Indians must have lived on this hill, planted crops, shot deer and small game. There's *got* to be arrowheads up here."—I, wanting to fulfill his expectation, bought arrowheads from an antique store and sneaked them up the hill where he would have to stumble upon them.

From Edgar's and my first meeting at the Paso Robles Inn, I'd felt the DNA, or whatever chemistry it is, that connects parent to child. Now I find we both like to trick loved ones by planting arrowheads for them to "discover." I'm speechless.

Back at Marilyn's house, she puts her arms around Edgar. "Show Margo the old album." I find glasses and bend over photos. They are of me, labeled in his hand "Little sweetheart," "My little Margo." Someone has torn out many photos; but many remain. How can I bear this, in Marilyn's house in Paso Robles: my wanting to throw my arms about my father's neck, his determination never to be alone with me?

It's time to leave.

They stand close together. Marilyn presents me with a box of See's candies, Edgar hands me a bottle of Paso Robles wine and then, incongruously, a package of two dozen toothbrushes. "My daughter Sharon gets these wholesale, we can't use them all." He pats my shoulder, escorts me to my rental car.

We stand close for a moment, we step away.

Driving south to Santa Barbara I bend double over the wheel with the most acute nausea I've ever experienced. Traffic's so heavy I can't stop, while to my right the Pacific slaps against a verge so densely littered with scrub, aluminum cans, garbage, plastic, wheel hubs, and McDonald's wrappers I can only imagine that if I get out of the car I'll be just another strangled woman in a black yard-bag for landscape-fill. I manage to make it to my pre-booked motel, crawl up the outside stairs. In the bathroom I am violently ill, vomiting until I cough up water. Afterwards, I shower, pick up the phone, and order a double gin and tonic delivered to my door.

The coastal restaurant food was not to blame. Those blandly civil sixteen hours with my father turned me inside out.

After the visit Edgar and I exchange letters. His is brief. "Thank you for giving me a truly noble experience. I have always loved you." I sign my letter "love," but cannot say I have always loved him, though our hours together are among the most important of my life. He dies a few years later—decisively, not lingering. Marilyn and his children quarrel over his ashes.

I have no claim.

They are all gone now.

In November 1972 Emma Merkel died of Alzheimers in a nursing home on Sturgeon Eddy Road, the West Side of Wausau she despised. I never went to see her. Yet ten years later I hang the photograph of the proud young Emma on my wall. I have been writing this narrative to discover why.

That landing she raved on should have been a stage, her audience applauding thousands. And what an actress she would have been! What eloquence, delivery, breath control, volume. What a Lady Macbeth, what a Phèdre. Like Sarah Siddons she would have ridden the high winds of tragedy. Like Mrs. Patrick Campbell, she would have thrust pins into her leading men. Like Sarah Bernhardt, she would have travelled the world with fifty pieces of luggage and a caged tiger. But, I am confident, she would have out-raptured them all. Instead, she wrote secret poetry, dreamed of romance and fame, married a meek man, bore children she did not know she did not want and—thwarted, baffled, ignorant and furious—made her family her captives and her role Destruction.

She fascinated me, she of the stained man's sweater with the missing buttons, she of the lilac perfume. Until this moment she has dominated my life.

Did I love her?

I believe I did.

But perhaps now she will leave me.

Made in the USA
Lexington, KY
17 August 2017